MAKING NEGOTIATIONS PREDICTABLE

MAKING NEGOTIATIONS PREDICTABLE

What Science Tells Us?

David De Cremer

China Europe International Business School (CEIBS), China

and

Madan M. Pillutla

London Business School (LBS), UK

palgrave
macmillan

First published 2012 by
PALGRAVE MACMILLAN

Palgrave Macmillan in the UK is an imprint of Macmillan Publishers Limited, registered in England, company number 785998, of Houndmills, Basingstoke, Hampshire RG21 6XS.

Palgrave Macmillan in the US is a division of St Martin's Press LLC, 175 Fifth Avenue, New York, NY 10010.

Palgrave Macmillan is the global academic imprint of the above companies and has companies and representatives throughout the world.

Palgrave® and Macmillan® are registered trademarks in the United States, the United Kingdom, Europe and other countries.

ISBN 978–1–137–02478–7

This book is printed on paper suitable for recycling and made from fully managed and sustained forest sources. Logging, pulping and manufacturing processes are expected to conform to the environmental regulations of the country of origin.

A catalogue record for this book is available from the British Library.

A catalog record for this book is available from the Library of Congress.

10   9   8   7   6   5   4   3   2   1
21 20 19 18 17 16 15 14 13 12

Printed and bound in Great Britain by
CPI Antony Rowe, Chippenham and Eastbourne

CONTENTS

CHAPTER 1

INTRODUCTION

Most people are familiar with the term 'negotiations'. The word is so often used in the media nowadays that it is almost impossible to avoid it. Newspapers and television cover many negotiations ranging from discussions about the responsibilities of each country for solving problems arising out of the financial crisis of 2008, to the necessary budget cuts within countries, to footballers and their agents negotiating contractual terms with teams. These examples, which come to mind when the term is introduced, obscure the fact that negotiations are not confined exclusively to financial matters or to the business world.

Our lives are made up of a succession of different negotiations – trying to get our children to do household chores, convincing our partners about whom we should invite to dinner, collaborating with a colleague on a project, and so on. These interactions, while not explicitly negotiations, deal with promises which have been made, emotions that have been experienced, and the rights and responsibilities attached to different people, and should therefore be considered to be negotiations. Viewed from this perspective, it is clear that even a simple decision, such as deciding whether or not to shake somebody's hand, is an act of negotiation. This is the position that we take in this book.

Negotiations are therefore not solely a matter for the professionals. It is something that we all deal with. Negotiation is an important part of our social interaction with others, not only in our professional lives, but also in our private lives. We humans are social creatures. The relationships we develop with other people in the course of our lives have an important influence on how we feel, think, and act. Most of these relationships are given shape and form through a process of mutual coordination – this type of coordination is closely linked to the art of negotiation.

Negotiation is the process by which two or more parties seek to approach a situation of potential conflict in a positive and constructive manner and reach an agreement which is acceptable to all sides. This description implies that negotiation – almost by definition – is focused on outcomes that you would not have been able to get on your own. The purpose of a negotiation is therefore to achieve a better outcome for all concerned than would otherwise have been possible without the negotiating process. Consequently negotiation is not a matter of 'winning', but rather a matter of reaching an agreement that is acceptable to all parties.

Even though negotiations are ideally a method to achieve constructive and positive results, it is not always easy to get all the relevant partners around the negotiating table, especially if there is no immediate problem. The first problem therefore is in getting people to realize the need for negotiations. If people do realize the need, it is often when there is conflict or a difference of opinion. The ability to overcome initial reservations and suspicions then becomes the first step in the negotiation process. These reservations and suspicions often colour discussions, leading to a lack of agreement even in situations where everyone is better off with one. Surely common sense should prevail so that agreement is reached quickly. That goes without saying, doesn't it? By their very presence everyone has indicated their willingness to negotiate, so is not the formal conclusion of the discussions just a matter of time? What could possibly go wrong?

Unfortunately things do not always work out this way. It is during the phase when discussions actually take place that the potential intractability of the situation often becomes most evident. When this happens the negotiations suddenly appear to be much more than a question of taking the time and making the effort to get the different parties around the negotiating table. While negotiations contain strong formal elements, which need to be followed up to structure efficient agreements, the rational approach is not sufficient to guarantee good outcomes. The idea that a rational approach on the part of the negotiating partners will quickly and automatically lead to clarity and an optimal solution has been shown to be a fallacy in practice. All too often, negotiations cannot be confined to rational and predictable procedures. They often lead to suboptimal solutions or even stalemates, from which no way out seems immediately possible. Dozens of recent national and international examples of failed negotiations can be cited to support this claim.

Take, for example, the issue of the sovereignty of the Falkland Islands. Argentina would like Great Britain to enter into talks to resolve what they see as the dispute over the sovereignty of the islands. Great Britain, on the other hand, sees no dispute. In early 2010 Hillary Clinton, the Secretary of State of the United States, decided to endorse Argentina's call for negotiations. In June of that same year the United States went a step further. It joined the Organisation of American States (OAS) in a unanimously passed voice vote resolution calling for negotiations between London and Buenos Aires. It was no surprise that this call was completely unacceptable to Great Britain. The fact that the resolution referred to the 'Malvinas' Islands, and not the Falkland Islands, its official, internationally recognized name, was a further insult. The British government issued a formal complaint over the use of the name 'Malvinas' at an official press conference. London also believed that it had been let down by its close partner America with whom it had a 'special relationship'. If the US commitment to this special relationship is sincere, then it should be clear to Washington that the backing they provided for negotiations is deeply unhelpful and unwelcome.

At other times, negotiations stall because of a misunderstanding between parties about the strength of the other side. The 2011 budget negotiations between the Obama-led White House and the Republicans offered an excellent example of such a misunderstanding. In the United States most Democrats think (probably correctly) that Republicans use tough negotiation tactics. For that reason many Democrats think that the use of an overly cautious negotiation style will not work. If you use such a style, you will get eaten by the other party. Unfortunately in the eyes of many Democrats and even of independents, President Obama engaged in using such a cautious style during the budget negotiations. Many of them were surprised to find out that their bottom line with respect to the debt ceiling was much different from the one being laid out by the president leading their charge.

Obama was criticized by his supporters for being too much of a nice guy and for trying to get along with the Republican leaders when they were clearly aggressive in pushing their agenda. At the same time the Republicans criticized Obama for being overly sensitive about policy differences. He was even blamed for being excessively devoted to his agenda about social justice and for continually using the code word 'fairness' in all of his arguments! Although the debt ceiling was raised in time, and the United States did not default on its obligations, rating agencies downgraded its credit rating. Of more importance is the fact that the leadership of the two major political parties was even more polarized by the budget negotiations and their relationship deteriorated on account of anger; this certainly does not bode well for future negotiations.

The year 2010 saw the start of one of the most long-drawn-out negotiations for the formation of a new government in the history of the world – the negotiation about a new Belgian government. On 13 June 2010 Belgian voters went to the polls. The result sent shockwaves through the Belgian political system. In Dutch-speaking Flanders, the nationalist New Flemish Alliance (N-VA) party of Bart De Wever became the largest party, while in French-speaking Wallonia the Socialist Party of Elio Di Rupo was able to dethrone the liberal Mouvement Réformateur (MR) from the leading position. Despite a number of positive signals during the initial stages of the negotiations, when De Wever and Di Rupo were still dealing with each other in a gentlemanly manner, the ideological waters separating the two parties were much too deep. Towards the end of 2010, the Flemish socialist Johan Vande Lanotte was appointed as an 'arbitrator', charged with bringing both sides closer together. The idea was to formulate a new law, which would grant greater fiscal autonomy to the regions (Flanders, Wallonia, and Brussels), which together make up the federal Belgian state. The resulting proposal was the subject of emotional comment and reaction on both sides of the linguistic divide. As a result, on 26 January 2011 Vande Lanotte tendered his resignation to the king. In February the liberal minister Reynders was asked to summarize the views of the different Belgian political parties. As expected, his efforts did not yield any progress. Just before Belgium celebrated its national bank holiday (21 June) some progress was finally made and eight parties embarked on a new journey to try to reconcile both social and economic differences by using a report written by the socialist Di Rupo, which ultimately led to the formation of a government at the end of December. All in all, it took the negotiators 541 days to reach an agreement – a world record almost unlikely to be ever broken.

The political world is not the only domain in which we find recent examples of suboptimal and irrational negotiations. The financial world is just as bad. In 2007 the Dutch Bank ABN-AMRO was taken over by a consortium of the Spanish bank Banco Santander, the Belgian bank Fortis and the Royal Bank of Scotland (RBS). This takeover marked the beginning of the end for the Belgian Fortis Bank and large financial problems for the other two banks. Numerous analysts have now concluded that the negotiations leading up to the deal were dominated more by emotion than by reason. The specific motivation behind the bid to acquire ABN AMRO is thought to be Maurice Lippens' (CEO of Fortis) desire to get back at the senior management of ABN AMRO, and particularly the CEO Rijkman

Groenink, for forcing Fortis to acquire another Belgian Bank at a vastly exaggerated expense in the 1990s (1). A motivation to get back at the other party cannot be considered to be a rational basis to conduct a negotiation.

These examples illustrate that negotiations frequently do not turn out the way people hope for or expect. More often than not, formal procedures and rational analyses are used to put the other party at a disadvantage, rather than to seek a mutually acceptable solution. Negotiators are frequently afflicted by negative stereotypes, emotional reactions to situations, and perceptions that do not match objective reality. As a consequence of these non-rational reactions it often happens that the parties involved in the negotiations have divergent views of the negotiation process and the outcomes that they are trying to achieve. This difference can sometimes be so wide that you might even think they came from a different planet!

THE MYTH OF THE RATIONAL NEGOTIATOR

The dominant perspective used to understand human behaviour in negotiation contexts is the notion of the 'rational actor'. This perspective holds that men (and women) are rational beings, who strive for the best possible outcomes for themselves and the parties they represent. To achieve their goals people use all available information accurately so that the resulting decisions cannot fail to be anything other than 'optimal'. An important consideration is that this strategy works because the other party also adopts the same logical approach. As a result of this belief in the power of reason there is a further belief that we will all be able to maintain our position within any given process of economic and/or social negotiation. However the examples cited above suggest that we should seriously doubt the validity of this belief.

A good illustration of the limitations of our rationality – in which the desire to secure one's own best interests is both acceptable and justified – can be found in the studies which make use of the so-called 'ultimatum game', which is a game that is extensively used in experimental economics research and is played between two contending parties (2). One of the players is given the role of 'giver' and decides how a particular sum (for example, 10 pound sterling or dollars) should be divided between himself or herself and the other player. The other player – known as the 'receiver' – is then offered a choice between two different decisions. He or she can either accept the division made by the giver (for example, seven pounds for the giver and three pounds for the receiver) or refuse. If the receiver accepts, the money will be divided in accordance with the giver's proposal. If he or she does not accept, both parties will receive nothing at all. According to the rational way of thinking, the giver should propose keeping the 9.99 pounds for himself or herself, offering just 0.01 cent to the receiver. Viewed logically the receiver should accept this offer, since 0.01 cent is still better than nothing – and since he or she began the game with nothing, he or she is still making a profit. The giver is behaving logically – seeking to maximize his or her own position – and we know that this behaviour is deemed to be acceptable within the precepts of this perspective. As you might expect, however, the results of the studies show that this is not what normally happens. In most cases the givers seek to achieve (as far as possible) a 50–50 split. And with some justification – since the vast majority of proposals which offer 20% or less to the receiver are rejected out of hand. Unequal distributions of this kind cause most people to react angrily against the 'unfairness' of the proposal. In other words the rational view of the human negotiator is not very efficient in terms of predicting likely outcomes.

It is now becoming clear that people do not always behave in a rational manner in negotiations. It is simply not true that people estimate with precision the best way to secure their own interests, whilst at the same time minimizing the risks of a stalemate. Many negotiations run into trouble precisely because they are confronted with the limits of human rationality. This explains why many negotiations fail to produce much in the way of mutually acceptable end results. People are *not* perfectly rational. We make mistakes and we allow ourselves to be led by our emotions, more often than we might think. In fact many of our decisions are not taken consciously at all, never mind rationally. A large number of our thoughts and actions are spontaneous and intuitive, and this has a major influence on our behaviour as a whole. For this reason it is vital that we understand exactly what rational thinking can accomplish – and what it cannot.

Does the fact that people do not behave rationally in a negotiation make negotiations a chaotic process where every attempt to predict others' behaviour is doomed to failure? The simple answer is no. There is a large body of research in psychology which can predict an individual's behaviour in specific circumstances with a great degree of accuracy. For example we know that people are more positive towards people who are similar to themselves. Negotiations between similar individuals should therefore lead to markedly different outcomes than those between dissimilar ones. Another example is that people react more negatively to losses than they react positively to gains. As a result we are motivated to avoid losses, even if it means taking great risks that could result in larger losses. We can therefore reliably say that negotiations over losses lead to more impasses than negotiations over the allocation of gains.

The aim of this book is to present research from social psychology and behavioural economics and to derive implications for negotiations. Both these fields primarily use experimental approaches to test different theories about human behaviour.

The studies that we will describe in this book are extremely useful in generating insights into human behaviour. What makes most of these studies useful is the fact that they have tried to map out the specific psychological tendencies which can cause our decisions to deviate systematically from what might be rationally expected. It is our conviction that this fundamental knowledge can and must be used to give us a better understanding of the sometimes seemingly incomprehensible aspects of negotiating behaviour. These same insights can also have a role in the daily negotiations with which we are all confronted, since they provide greater awareness of our own behaviour and help us to better interpret the behaviour of others. This approach is based on a very simple idea. If we want to achieve optimal results in negotiating situations, it is necessary for us to understand why people do the things that they do. In this respect the social sciences have a very important role to play.

This scientific approach has considerable external validity. Learning to understand what drives and motivates humans at their most basic level will help us to predict how they are likely to react in more complex situations.

WHAT THIS BOOK IS ABOUT

There are many books in the market about how negotiations ought to be conducted. These books provide a sound framework and empirically validated principles about how one must conduct negotiations. We have read many of these books and can recommend those by Leigh Thompson (3), Howard Raiffa (4), Deepak Malhotra and Max Bazerman (5), and Richard Shell (6) as exemplary, as they rely upon psychological and economics research to provide a robust guide for action.

Where our book differs from these books is in our focus on understanding important psychological elements in negotiations. These elements include notions of trust, fairness, power, intuitions, emotions, cognitive and motivational biases, and situational framing. Most people will recognize these as important issues in negotiations and often as the reason why negotiations are successful or fail. Take the example of the Falkland Islands that we discussed before. These negotiations have stalled on account of the lack of trust between the two principals involved. Similarly the Belgian negotiations failed on account of the differing perceptions of what was fair among the contending parties.

While these topics are covered in the books that we recommend above, we move them to the centre stage here and discuss what negotiators can learn from social psychological research on these topics.

The attentive reader will comment (and rightly) that negotiations are more than a simple matter of psychology. An understanding of structures and procedures that help create value is still necessary to be a successful negotiator. The purpose of this book is *not* to give a detailed, step-by-step analysis of negotiating procedures. The existing literature has already covered this subject more than thoroughly. Instead our intention is to shed more light on a number of psychological processes and phenomena which can have a direct or indirect effect on negotiating behaviour. We are often unaware of particular habits or behaviours which encourage us to act irrationally rather than rationally towards our negotiating partners. We will therefore deal with chapters related to the structure and procedures of negotiations in the Chapter 2 before launching into the meat of the book, which is a discussion of social psychological research that is relevant to negotiations.

The book is organized as follows. In Chapter 2 we will discuss important structural and procedural elements of negotiations. We will then move on to discussing cognitive and motivational biases in Chapter 3. Chapter 4 deals with emotions and intuitions. Chapter 5 discusses how the frames that people use in negotiation situations affect the outcomes of negotiations. Chapters 6–8 deal with the important issues of trust, power, and fairness. The chapters have been written such that the reader can read any one of them independently or in any sequence after reading Chapter 2.

CHAPTER 2

NEGOTIATION BASICS: STRUCTURE AND PROCESS

In this chapter we will introduce basic structural and procedural elements of all negotiations. It is important to have a sound grasp of these elements because the single biggest determinant of negotiator success is how well prepared you are for a negotiation. The ideas introduced in this chapter will enable you to plan properly for the negotiation.

The negotiation process consists of two distinct phases: preparation and implementation. Most experts agree that preparation is the most important determinant of negotiation success. Negotiators who are well prepared have a chance to do well even if they are not quite good at table tactics. But even the most charming individual will not get a good negotiation outcome if he or she is not prepared. You cannot just 'start' negotiations from scratch or conjure them up out of thin air. You first need to clearly analyse the situation. But what factors should you take into consideration?

The first and most important factor is your objective for the negotiation – and the price that you are prepared to pay to achieve your objectives. Clarity about objectives seems like an obvious idea, yet it is surprising how often we do not know exactly what we want from a negotiation. When we are clear about our objectives, we tend to stop our preparation unfortunately. Why unfortunately? Because all too often negotiators fail to examine the needs and objectives of their negotiation counterparty. Taking their needs into consideration allows you to plan the trade-offs that you need to make in order to reach an agreement that is good for all sides.

You need to consider the following essential elements of a negotiation when preparing for one:

- You – your bargaining style, objectives and expectations.
- The other party – their style, their objectives and expectations.
- Alternatives – both yours and the other side's.

These elements interact with one another to determine the structure of the negotiations and the procedures that you need to follow. Preparation is about understanding the game that you are playing and matching your negotiation tactics with the situation.

Let's briefly analyse these elements and understand how they affect the negotiation process starting with alternatives.

BEST ALTERNATIVE TO NEGOTIATED AGREEMENT

Negotiations seldom go the way you had hoped. You do not always get what you want or ask for. For this reason, it is important to know in advance what you will do if the negotiations do not allow you to

reach your objectives. The way to do this is to identify alternatives that are not dependent upon the
successful completion of this negotiation. The best
of these alternatives is often referred to as the best
alternative to a negotiated agreement or BATNA for
short. A good BATNA gives you the security of a viable
reserve position on which you can fall back if the current negotiations break down. A BATNA can also help
you to decide whether or not to accept a particular
proposal put forward by the other side. If you have a
strong alternative, your opponents will need to make
a very good offer before you feel obliged to accept.
For this reason, however, it is also important that you
should never reveal your BATNA to outsiders. This is
a technique often used by salesmen: if they can discover your BATNA, they know exactly how to make
their pitch. Once you have indicated your intention
to make a purchase, the first question they will usually
ask you is: how large is your budget? Never answer this
question! This would be giving away just how much –
or how little – room for manoeuvre you have at your
disposal. The best way to respond to this question is
with another question: make clear that your answer
depends on what the seller has to offer. This puts the
ball back in his or her court, so that you can see just
how much room for manoeuvre he or she has!

THE BOTTOM LINE

It is also important for a negotiator to be aware of the
final offer that he or she would be prepared to accept.
The bottom line is informed by the alternative but also
takes into account transaction costs. For example if
the best alternative to the car that I am negotiating

over is one that is in a dealership a few miles away, then I can take into the account the costs that I will incur in taking up the alternative and will therefore be willing to pay a little more for the car in the dealership that I am currently at. If you are a seller, the bottom line means the lowest price that you would be willing to offer in order to make a sale. If you are a buyer, it means the highest price that you are willing to pay in order to make a purchase. Once this boundary is clear, it also makes it easier to decide when negotiations should be opened or drawn to a close. Of course, it is not always easy to know where this final limit should be set. Depending upon the type of negotiations in which you are involved, you may be required to consider a lesser or greater number of relevant factors. This may mean that in some circumstances you need to take account of several different scenarios, whereas in other circumstances a single scenario will be sufficient. In any case, it is important that you set a bottom line and stick to it. Oftentimes the negotiation dynamics are such that people lose sight of what is a good outcome in a negotiation and aim merely to reach an agreement. In these instances the goal becomes one of trying to reach an agreement rather than to reach a good deal. Having a bottom line that is sacrosanct prevents us from doing a bad deal.

ZONE OF POSSIBLE AGREEMENT

As soon as you know your own bottom line and have an estimate of the bottom line of the other party, you can decide whether or not you have any negotiating space. Negotiators refer to this as the zone of possible agreement or ZOPA for short. The ZOPA contains within it all the different agreements which are acceptable to both sides. Imagine that you want to buy a house with an asking price of 200,000 pounds. You make an offer of 180,000 pounds. It is possible that the owner may be willing to sell the house for a minimum price of 185,000 pounds, whereas you would be prepared to go as a far as 192,000 pounds to secure the home of your dreams. In this scenario, there is therefore negotiating space between 185,000 pounds and 192,000 pounds. Any offer that falls within this range is likely to be accepted. Of course, the object of the exercise is to obtain the most advantageous price for yourself. If you are the seller, you will be looking towards the upper end of the negotiating space. If you are the buyer, you will be more interested in the lower limit. This is an example of positive negotiating space, since in this instance there is still room to negotiate. However, you may well be confronted with a situation in which there is negative negotiating space. Take for example a situation where your highest offer is 180,000 pounds, while the owner is not prepared to settle for a cent less than 185,000 pounds. In such a scenario, it is important that both parties should adopt a cooperative attitude, and check whether the limits that they have set are indeed the correct ones. Sometimes the intervention of a third party can be useful in helping to verify these limits. This third party must seek to fix an objective figure that can be regarded as acceptable by both parties as their new final limit. The third party can also encourage both sides to be more open in their approach to the negotiations, either by talking to them jointly or by acting as an intermediary for the communication of their respective opinions.

DISTRIBUTIVE VERSUS INTEGRATIVE NEGOTIATIONS

Once you have determined what your alternatives are and fixed your bottom line and have also tried to understand your counterparty's alternatives, then you will need to determine what kind of a negotiation you are in.

There are mainly two kinds of negotiation situations: distributive and integrative. In a distributive negotiation, there is usually a single issue at stake (or if there are multiple issues, all parties to the negotiation care equally about these issues) and there is no scope for gains in trade; whatever one side gains, the other side loses. Since this is analogous to the situation where two individuals divide a limited resource between them, such as a pie, this is sometimes called a 'fixed pie' negotiation (or a 'zero-sum game'). Simple price negotiations, such as haggling in marketplaces, are distributive. An integrative situation offers the potential for different outcomes to be suggested and generated because more than one issue is involved and parties put different weights on each issue. Trade-offs can be made, based on the relative importance of the different issues to each party. Most negotiations where there are many factors involved, or there is the potential for different outcomes to achieve the same goals, are integrative. If they appear to be distributive at first glance, you may want to spend some time figuring out if you can change it into an integrative situation.

The process of agreeing a price for a house seems at first glance to be distributive. There are two sides in the negotiation. The buyer wants the price as low as possible and the seller wants it as high as possible. With the estate agent's valuation as the starting point, negotiations begin, typically through the procedure of the buyer offering increasing prices until the seller accepts one (or either side gives up and walks away). Other factors may come to bear on this negotiation: the need for the seller to complete the sale within a particular timescale (perhaps to obtain money to pay for his or her new house), the need for the buyer to move in on a particular date (perhaps because of the sale of his or her own house), the need for the seller to move out on a particular date (into his or her new house), the option to include appliances and soft furnishings in the sale of the house and so on.

Clearly, there are potentially more issues to this negotiation than just price. Whether they are used in discussions governs the nature of the negotiation. If information is shared between the parties, the negotiation can become more integrative. There is the potential for different options to be explored, trade-offs made and a solution reached that satisfies both parties.

TRY TO UNDERSTAND THE NEEDS OF THE OTHER PARTY

As noted in the Introduction most negotiators focus too closely on their own position (7). This is a very human failing, but it is one that can be very damaging to the negotiation process. Research indicates that this can work strongly against you. Various studies have shown that negotiators who think more deeply about the different alternatives which the other party might put forward are often better able to obtain a more beneficial counterproposal as a result (8). Maintaining a perspective which embraces not only your own requirements but also the requirements of others creates additional value. The combination of both perspectives helps to prevent the negotiations from getting bogged down in the myth of the 'fixed pie' (see Chapter 3). This is a situation in which both parties – assuming they fail to take account of each other's position – want to keep the 'pie' of potential negotiating gains at its existing size, rather than looking for different, perhaps smaller, alternatives.

Failure to consider the motives of your negotiating partner can trigger a number of other human reactions which can be equally damaging to the negotiating process. Many academic papers demonstrate that focusing too much on your own wishes can lead you to ignore or overlook valuable information – both explicit and implicit – which the other negotiating partners are trying to communicate (9, 10). This means that you will be less quick to notice the strengths and weaknesses of these partners (11). Worse still, this limited perception will encourage you to consistently attach less value to the concessions which the other side are willing to make – whereas in reality the proposal might actually be quite a good one (12).

In other words, assessing the motives of everyone involved in the negotiations is an important step which should not be omitted or glossed over. This may sound like stating the obvious, but it is surprising how often this seemingly simple step causes problems or is performed inadequately. Many negotiators have a tendency to go in search of the least useful information about their negotiating partners. For example, they attach great importance to information about the personality of their 'opponents' and often attribute their actions to aspects of this subjective personality, rather than to other more objective, external factors (13).

It is almost as if we are preprogrammed to try and find out what kind of person our negotiating partner is. Sometimes this can be a good strategy – but often it is not. It is crucial to remember that the situation in its broadest sense often has a greater impact on the behaviour of a person than the narrow dictates of their own personality. If this is the case, then the behaviour in question is no longer diagnostic evidence for assessing that person's personality, since it is determined by circumstances rather than character. Similar mistakes are often made during the negotiations themselves. Too much weight is attached to what the other person says and does, rather than focusing on what this person is actually trying to achieve. In reality, this latter type of strategic and objective information is much more valuable. Knowing what motives your negotiating opponent is actually pursuing will allow you to better predict his or her likely behaviour than simply knowing what kind of person he or she is. Nevertheless, research is clear on the relative precedence of these two different types of information: knowledge of the other person's BATNA is a much more effective way to read your negotiating partner's thoughts than knowledge of his or her personality (14).

In short, it is important that a negotiator should not worry too much about the personalities of the other people sitting around the negotiating table. It is more useful to understand their underlying motivation – and turn this to your advantage. You can reach this situation by asking yourself questions which puts you in the other person's shoes. For example, you can ask yourself what you would do if his or her BATNA was your BATNA. Or how you would approach the negotiations if you knew that the other person had a reputation as either a 'hard' or a 'soft' negotiator. By asking questions of this kind, you can soon work out the kind of information that you need to use to make your own decisions. If you find that you are relying too heavily on information that is strongly personality-based, then it is time to refocus your attention on the needs and objectives that really make your negotiating adversary tick. Because you can be fairly certain that he or she will be doing precisely the same thing for you!

Another key question is how you can best obtain reliable information about the other negotiators. In this respect, it is important that you should obtain your information from a variety of sources. All too often, information is communicated with a particular – and not necessarily objective – purpose in mind. Even if each of the multiple sources is biased, getting the information from multiple sources will result in a more accurate understanding of the other party as long as the multiple sources are independent of one another. The information you acquire also allows you to check whether someone is trying to pull wool over your eyes. Some people, unfortunately, view negotiations as situations in which ordinary notions of ethical and moral behaviour don't apply. So, many negotiators have come to see hidden agendas to be an integral part of the negotiating process (15). Research has shown that people who lie about their BATNA often achieve better negotiating results – but only if the lie remains concealed (16). If the deceit is discovered, it seems that it is easier to 'forgive and forget' if the 'liar' is one of the weaker partners (17). Even so, the message is clear: do not allow yourself to be surprised by the hidden agendas of the other people at the negotiating table. And to make sure that this does not happen, try and get to know these people as well as you possibly can in advance, by every direct and indirect means at your disposal.

Information search does not end with the preparation period. A good negotiator is constantly updating his or her ideas about the other party and about the ZOPA based on interactions with the counterparty. Some observers characterize a negotiator as a detective.

THE NEGOTIATOR AS DETECTIVE

The act of negotiating and its preceding preparations are not isolated activities carried out in a vacuum. For this reason, it is advisable to keep your eyes and ears open for useful information which may become available during the course of the negotiations. New information can help you to adjust your strategy, if necessary. And often it is indeed necessary. Negotiations are sometimes conducted in a much less structured manner than you may have anticipated. This unexpected dynamic can easily lead to misunderstandings and can result in developments which you had not foreseen in advance. For this reason, it is vital that you should be willing to question your own assumptions as the negotiations progress, so that you can make any changes that may be necessary to meet new circumstances. Do negotiators do this enough? Regrettably not! We know that people are more inclined to opt for the easiest solution and this often means clinging on to the old, familiar ways of working (a preference for the *status quo*). People are quickly satisfied with the things that they know, and so seldom bother to look for information that changes their initial judgements. Various studies have shown that the majority of negotiators do not make optimal use of the information which becomes available during the course of the negotiation process. They prefer to restrict themselves to tried and trusted partners and to well-known channels of communication, rather than to explore the possibilities offered by new contacts and new sources (18).

To become a successful negotiator, it is essential to adopt the constantly critical attitude of a researcher. In recent negotiation literature, this attitude has been compared to that of a detective. A negotiator needs a very well-developed sense of curiosity, an attitude of openness towards unknown and sometimes unwelcome information. This is not so very different from the methods used by scientific and academic researchers. You behave like a detective who uses a particular method to solve the 'mystery' of why your negotiating partner behaves as he or she does. For this reason, it is also important to be sufficiently aware of the irrational tendencies which affect the behaviour of every negotiator. This knowledge will allow you to analyse each new negotiating situation more critically and with a sharper focus.

It frequently happens that we fail to understand the decisions taken by our negotiating partners. As a result, we have developed a tendency to explain their behaviour in prejudicial ways. Instead, it is important for negotiators to continue asking 'why' questions about this behaviour. By working in this systematic manner, it should be possible, for example, to discover why the other party feels uncomfortable or what will make it easier for him or her to accept your proposal. In short, you must try to find out whether the behaviour, which may seem strange at first glance, is really just a strategic ploy or whether it has some other, deeper origin.

Starting from this idea of the negotiator as a detective, it is possible to describe three different avenues of approach. These suggestions are based on recent work by Malhotra and Bazerman (5).

1. *Don't just discuss the demands of the opposing party, but try to find out why these demands are important to him or her.* Many negotiations grind to a halt because of constant references to demands: not only the demands of the other party, but also your own demands. This emphasis on what everyone wants often leads us to overlook the reasons why we actually want it. Why will one side stick to a particular demand like a limpet to a rock? This question often remains unasked. Or if it is asked, the answer remains unknown. And as we all know, unknown is often unloved. The consequences are not difficult to imagine. Both sides are soon accusing the other of making unreasonable claims, whilst ignoring their own much more reasonable position. If this type of discussion persists for too long, the result will be a stalemate

from which there is no escape. To some extent, this escalation can be avoided if we make more of an effort to find out why particular demands are non-negotiable for one of the parties. If you can actually discover the answer to this question, it can lead to a different kind of discussion, a discussion in which prejudices and prior assumptions can be put to one side, so that a more positive and creative approach can emerge. This makes it easier to identify alternative options which may never have been considered before. More importantly, these options may have the advantage of being able to satisfy the objectives of the opposing party, but in a different way. This can help to reopen (and even solve) problems that were previously incapable of discussion – and so prevent them from disrupting further progress of the wider negotiating process.

2. *Try to discover the limits of the opposing party – and also how you can help him or her to move beyond those limits.* Negotiators often complain that they are hampered by the limits set by the other parties in the process, which allow them very little room for manoeuvre. For example, political negotiators will often argue that they cannot possibly accept this or that proposal, because they would simply not be able to sell it to their grass-roots supporters. Similarly, house sellers often act in accordance with a whole series of limits by which they feel bound. Sometimes these limits can be relatively trivial. For example, the seller may not want to vacate his or her property at an earlier date – which may be more convenient for the buyer – because he or she has still not found a new property to live in. However, few people make any serious effort to discover

the real reasons behind these limits. As a result, the opportunity is often missed to find an alternative solution which may be acceptable to the other party. For example, the buyer might know an estate agent who has properties for sale in the area to which the seller is hoping to move. The failure to explore these possibilities more fully can lead to frustration and even to a breakdown in the negotiations. And an inability to understand why the other person is setting these limits can often provoke a hostile and defensive reaction. For this reason, it is important to ask questions which will help you to discover why your negotiating partner is seemingly not willing to allow you more breathing space. These questions will help to bring both sides closer together and will encourage them to search for mutually acceptable alternative solutions which have not been previously considered. Of course, this requires a cooperative attitude from all concerned. And this attitude is more difficult to achieve once the importance of the negotiations and the differences between the parties become greater.

3. *Even though the negotiations may seem to be going nowhere, keep on negotiating!* Once it appears that the negotiations are not going to lead to the desired result, the willingness to discuss further can quickly fade. At the same time, the willingness to see things from the other person's point of view also decreases. 'What does it really matter?' you might say. 'The whole business is already doomed to failure, isn't it?' This is faulty reasoning. It is always useful – and of great strategic importance – to keep on asking yourself why the other party is behaving in a particular manner. In many fields of life –

politics, business, sport – you will be confronted with the same negotiating partners on more than one occasion. Your negotiations may have failed this time, but the lessons you have learnt about these partners may help you to succeed next time – to your own best advantage. For this reason, the best strategy is always to keep on asking questions, even if the negotiations seem to be going badly wrong. This should at least provide you with an explanation for the failure – and it is precisely this information, and the understanding which it brings, which may help you to make progress in the future. In this respect, it is also important to remember that people tend to become more talkative and more open-hearted once a negotiation process seems to be approaching the point of collapse. This will often make it easier to identify what is truly important to them and what their key motives really are. Once nothing seems to be left at stake – 'the deal has gone anyway' – the discussions become less competitive. This change in perception causes people to lower their guard, so that they now share information that they would not have been willing to receive at the height of the discussions (also see Chapter 5 on framing effects).

BUT, THEIR PROBLEMS ARE NOT YOUR PROBLEMS

While it is important to take the other party's needs into consideration in negotiations, it is not a good idea to own their problems. The other side may try to make you an unwitting partner in their problems. Signalling their own problems in this way is often used as an excuse to explain why they cannot agree with what you want. Many of these problems may seem trivial, and scarcely related to the main topics of negotiation between the parties. Even so, this information can influence you in a manner which is hard for you to assess accurately. The aim of this tactic is to try and make their problems your problems as well – including the emotional context in which these problems are framed. It is almost as if they are trying to infect you with their own ideas.

Studies have indeed shown that the longer you are exposed to something, the more likely you are to evaluate it positively (19). By becoming more and more familiar with the problems of the other party, you run the risk of becoming increasingly sympathetic towards those problems. For this reason, it is important that you should not absorb – or be absorbed by – the difficulties which your negotiating opponent claims to be facing. If you fail to do this, you will find it much harder to put him or her under pressure during the later stages of the discussions. You will be less decisive than might otherwise have been the case. But does this mean that you should not listen to your opponent? Surely it is important to know what he or she is thinking? Indeed it is, and I have already mentioned the necessity of trying to look at things from the other person's point of view. However, it is equally important to remember that you should only do this with the express purpose of obtaining a better understanding of the aims and behaviour of your negotiating partners. This is a purely rational process: you must not adopt an emotional perspective. If you do, you will soon find yourself sailing in very dangerous waters. Try to remain as objective as possible and view all the emotional information offered by the other side in terms of what it can do for you. How can you use it? What benefits might this yield? However, if it becomes clear that your knowledge of the problems faced by the other side is only likely to complicate your own decision-making process, it is probably wiser to ignore this kind of information completely.

HOW DO YOU WANT TO COME ACROSS?

Another important element that you should consider is how you want to come across in the negotiation. The manner in which you conduct your negotiations has a significant influence on the final outcome and on your level of satisfaction with that outcome. Failure to have a clear understanding about how the negotiating process should progress can often lead to a breakdown before concrete results are in sight. This leads to an inevitable question: How exactly should this process be conducted? How should the agenda for discussion be agreed? How should information be exchanged? How should decisions be taken? How can the relationship between the different parties involved be strengthened?

We now know that people are not only motivated by the value of the results they can achieve. Non-economic factors can sometimes act as even stronger motives. Research indicates that the manner in which decisions are taken is often as important as the end result (20). In fact, a positive perception of the decision-making process can actually make it easier to accept negative outcomes. How is this possible?

Studies into the concept of 'fairness' have shown that the use of an 'honest' decision-making process (the provision of accurate information, the chance to express opinions freely, the use of transparent and consistent procedures, the option for subsequent amendment of the decisions, etc.) gives a feeling of control to all the parties involved. This feeling has an instrumental function. It ensures that the negotiations take place within a less uncertain framework. However, the use of these procedures also has a non-instrumental function, in the sense that they help to determine how each of the parties will feel they have been treated. The use of fair and open procedures signals that each party is being properly respected, and that they are regarded as worthy partners for negotiation. This relational message – which is implicit in the use of correct procedures – serves to strengthen the mutual relations between the negotiators. Moreover, because the procedures have both an instrumental and a non-instrumental function, the level of mutual trust and confidence will also increase and will lend added legitimacy to the negotiations. This is crucial: negotiations must be seen as legitimate, since this will encourage the parties to commit themselves more readily to the agreed need to find a satisfactory final solution.

In other words, the process phase is just as important as the phase in which the end result is achieved. However, this involves more than simply guaranteeing the honesty and transparency of the procedures. Procedures which are used correctly will certainly help to create the necessary commitment to the negotiation process. But it is also vital that this accumulated commitment is properly managed. A high level of cohesion between the negotiators can make it easier to agree precisely how the procedures should be used. This in turn means that it must be possible to apply the procedures with sufficient flexibility. For example, it may be desirable, depending upon the circumstances, that some decisions are taken in parallel (i.e., at the same time) and others sequentially (i.e., not at the same time). The procedures must also be capable of adaptation if it becomes clear that other pathways might lead to better end results or to results that are at least equivalent to what the parties had in mind at the beginning of the negotiating process.

Negotiators also need to know who they should come across in a negotiation. Is it important to show that you are not a pushover? Is it better to try and be friendly to disarm the other person? As with so many other things in life, the best option is actually a combination of both approaches. As one of the great negotiation scholars Keith Murnighan often says, the best strategy is to have: 'An iron fist in a velvet glove.'

What does this mean? It means that one should be firm in pursuing one's goals, but should do so in a gentle and polite fashion. This style also means that that you are clear about matters on which you are actually prepared to negotiate on and those on which you can't afford to compromise. On the issues that you are willing to concede, you can show a willingness to discuss points of difference and even give in to the demands of the other side. The demonstration of this willingness helps the other side understand that you are someone they can do business with, someone who can make concessions without wanting the world in return. On those issues where you are not prepared to compromise, you need to be firm. By sending a strong signal in this manner, you show where your own lower limits are set, but without appearing to be unreasonable. Remember that people do not like uncertainty. Consequently, it is important to give others certainty about what you want and what you don't want. This will keep the negotiations focused and transparent.

The iron fist–velvet glove approach also has other significant advantages. It can help you to present your negotiating credentials to the other parties in the most positive light. By making clear what you limits are and by sticking to them, you create an impression of consistency. Consistency makes your behaviour and your decision-making more 'predicable'. In turn, this makes your negotiating partners more comfortable, since you are less likely to spring any unwelcome surprises. Of course, this 'predictable' aspect of your negotiating style will only be of benefit to you if you do not apply it in a naive manner that allows you to be easily exploited. Being predictable is not effective if it means that your thinking becomes rigid, so that you will not change your behaviour even when it becomes necessary. In this case, you would be an easy target for the manipulations of the other side.

Consistency also has the advantage that it encourages other people to regard you as honest, as a man (or woman) of integrity (21). If your negotiating partner thinks that you are honest, his or her decision-making is more likely to be influenced by the principle of reciprocity: giving something in return for favours granted. Because of your honest reputation, he or she will respond by becoming more honest and more positive in his or her own behaviour (we will discuss this in more detail in Chapter 6).

Finally, an attitude which removes all uncertainty with regard to your own position – what you want and what you don't want – will also increase your own self-confidence. Providing this does not tip over into arrogance, self-confidence is an important weapon in the negotiator's armoury. It gives the impression to others that you are a strong and stable person – and these qualities make you more attractive and more charismatic (22, 23). This has the important advantage of increasing your influence during the negotiating process. By exuding self-confidence, you will convince your negotiating partners that you possess the necessary competencies and personal qualities to bring the negotiations to a successful conclusion.

DON'T BE AFRAID TO ASK

By now, it should be clear that you need to assume that every party will prepare its negotiating position meticulously. Consequently, the other side will also have had the opportunity to devise a strategy which they believe will allow them reach their objectives. Likewise, it is your responsibility as a negotiator to ensure that your own objectives are satisfactorily fulfilled. For this reason (as we have previously said), it is important to learn as much as you can about the other people at the negotiating table. This in turn implies that one of the key skills of a negotiator must be the willingness and the ability to ask questions. Questions which make the intentions of your opponents that much clearer. Questions which can reveal their current attitudes and emotional state of mind. Questions which make their promises more concrete. Although it might seem obvious that questions of this kind need to be asked, many negotiators do not feel comfortable with this aspect of their task. They have difficulty accepting the idea that the other side will give you something – information, a proposal a promise – simply because you ask.

And so they don't ask. In addition, they also believe that listening – and the related creation of pauses of silence – is a better tactic, since it encourages the other side to keep talking. This may lead them into overstepping the mark, almost tricking them into making commitments which they cannot later retract, except with great difficulty and loss of face. Nevertheless, there is also a drawback to this tactic. If you allow too many silences during the discussions, the other side will quickly realize what you are doing and will clam up completely – increasing the likelihood of a stalemate from which no one will benefit.

As a consequence of the above 'prejudices', most negotiators ask too few questions. And if they do ask questions, they tend to be general rather than specific. However, there are two very good reasons which show why asking questions is always better than not asking questions. The first reason can be summed up in the words of the popular saying: 'If you don't ask, you won't get.' This is simple common sense. If you fail to ask for the things that you want, you can hardly expect the other side to just give them to you. Moreover, studies show that people are continually amazed just how much they are given, if they only have the courage to ask. However, this is only the case if the questions are well prepared and properly put.

These arguments make clear that you should not regard the asking of questions as a problem. On the contrary, it should become your second nature. Once again, however, you should be aware that this broad general statement is subject to a number of conditions. First and foremost, you should not underestimate the amount of preparation required. You need to know exactly what you want to achieve and how this can be realized within the context of the current discussions. Only then will you be able to ask the right questions at the right time. If you know why you are asking a particular price or making a particular offer, it can do no harm to communicate this information to the other side in unambiguous terms. By making concrete statements and asking well-formulated questions, you will create an impression of sincerity and competence. Being perceived as competent is particularly important in helping you to achieve the results you want. This has also been confirmed by research, which shows that negotiators who define their goals in precise (as opposed to vague) terms perform better and are much more likely to reach their objectives. Being concrete about why you are pursuing a particular aim can also help you to formulate ambitious targets. And ambitious targets are also important, since they can motivate people to commit fully to a particular line of action. Studies into the formulation of objectives have revealed that people are more intrinsically motivated and more prepared to make greater efforts on behalf of objectives that are slightly more difficult than expected (24). Consequently, it is useful to realize that you should not be afraid to ask that little bit more of people. The only caveat is that you need to know exactly what you are doing – and why.

A second important condition for success is the need to show proper respect for your negotiating partner. It is always easier to ask questions in an atmosphere of mutual respect. You can achieve this by showing due courtesy and deference for the values which you know are important to the other side. Or by expressing appreciation for what they have achieved in the past. Top negotiators have the ability to talk amicably with their opponents on everyday matters, while still disagreeing fundamentally on the matters which are important. For this reason, it can do no harm to begin the negotiations with a polite enquiry about the health or family situation of the other people at the negotiating table. This mark of respect increases the likelihood that you will be granted more room for manoeuvre to ask the questions that really count. At the same time, respect also implies that you must know when to stop asking for more. This is particularly important if you anticipate the need to negotiate further with the same people at some future date. You may have achieved your objectives this time, but if your partners see you as 'pushy' or 'greedy', you may not be quite so lucky next time.

WHY A DEADLINE IS OFTEN NOT A DEADLINE

We all have busy agendas. However, many people make use of the chaos in their personal planning to reduce the time which they make available for negotiating the things that are really important to you. This can lead to stress and frustration. You may begin to doubt whether or not you have sufficient time to do justice to the interests which you are seeking to defend. As a result, your surprise – and relief! – will no doubt be considerable when you discover that your negotiating partner suddenly manages to find an extra hour or two, so that the discussions can be properly rounded off. This simple decision will magically improve the atmosphere and smooth the way towards a mutually acceptable solution. But why could he or she not have said this in the first place?

The decision of the other party to stay on and negotiate a little longer has a strategic aspect to it.

It signals that he or she has respect for you and is genuinely interested in your views. As a result, you – and other negotiators in a similar position – may be inclined to feel flattered by the granting of this extra time. It is a simple tactic, but an effective one: by making you feel good, he or she hopes to get something in return. This idea of implicitly paying your negotiating partner a compliment – providing it is done correctly – can often pay dividends in the long term. Research has confirmed that people who receive a compliment regard the giver of that compliment with greater esteem, feel a greater degree of emotional attachment towards him or her and experience a general improvement in the all-round negotiating atmosphere (25, 26). The use of compliments is therefore an important social weapon which can help you to achieve your desired results (27).

Put simply, the gradual granting of more and more time to complete the negotiations can frequently result in the other side becoming more motivated to accept your proposals. Consequently, this tactic can be compared with the so-called foot-in-the-door sales technique (28). Initially, you open the door just a little bit – making just a few hours available for a relatively short negotiating session. Later, you can open the door a little wider, by agreeing to extend the length of this initial session or by making an appointment for a new one. In this way, it seems as if you are slowly giving the other side more and more time to make their point. In exchange for this 'concession', the other side will be inclined to regard you in a more positive and more constructive light for the remainder of the negotiations. If this tactic works, it should allow you to penetrate the negotiating defences of your opponents more quickly and more easily, so that you are better able to achieve your own objectives.

In view of the potential effectiveness of this tactic – and as with many of the other tactics we have discussed so far – it is important to be aware of the extent to which the other side may be trying to employ this weapon against you! As mentioned, the granting of more time may make you better disposed towards your negotiating partner. For this reason, it is important that you should not regard any change in the negotiating agenda as some kind of personal favour. In most cases, the other side will already have planned to extend the available time before the meeting even began. Remember also that by allowing you a little extra time, the other person is, nonetheless, surreptitiously trying to force you to come to a deal more quickly than you might like. He or she knows that people have a tendency to round off negotiations as quickly as possible, particularly if time is short ('agreement bias': see Chapters 3 and 5). To avoid this pitfall, it is important to make clear that you will only be making your decision after the meeting – and not during the meeting. If the extension of the length of the meeting was just a tactic, the other party will most probably not push the matter any further and in all likelihood will end the discussions at the time originally planned.

CHAPTER 3

COGNITIVE ERRORS OF NEGOTIATORS

9 December 2011 will go down as a red letter day in the United Kingdom's 38-year membership of the European Community, and latterly Union. David Cameron, the prime minister of the United Kingdom, used his veto and refused to sign a new intergovernmental accord designed to save the euro. He thought that he had the support of many of the other member states including Hungary, but found himself to be alone in refusing to sign the accord. The talks broke down when Cameron failed to get the assurances he was seeking for the City of London and Britain's place in the single market. The prime minister insisted upon a legally binding 'protocol' to protect the City from more European Union (EU) financial regulations. He didn't get one so he blocked a deal. Many observers noted that the British prime minister overplayed his hand, either because he overestimated his support or because he underestimated European leaders' fears about the euro. As a result of his veto, said *The Guardian* (December 10, 2011), 'the UK is now likely to be out of the loop at the outset of crucial EU debates for years to come. Our partners now have a forum in which to seal alliances on single-market

issues in advance of votes being taken. But the UK will be locked out.'

What explains Cameron's overconfidence? Was he promised support that eventually did not materialize? Or, as is more likely the case, did he see what he wanted to see and ignore vital information that could have told him that he was on the wrong course?

When negotiations fail to go as well as expected, as above, it is noticeable that each of the parties will have a different explanation for why things went wrong. Moreover, it is striking to note that each side will strongly deny that they have been guilty of irrational thinking. Perhaps these reactions are not so surprising. The majority of the cognitive errors made by negotiators are made subconsciously. They are not errors that can be directly cited as the reason why a particular bad decision was taken. Their effect is much more insidious and can damage the negotiating process as a whole. For this reason, it is important that negotiators should have a good understanding of these psychological pitfalls, which can also be referred to as negotiating fallacies.

The recognition that negotiators are unconsciously influenced by both their own thoughts and the situation in which they find themselves in is an important first step. But in what way is this concept new? As already mentioned in our introductory chapter, the way in which we look at decisions is strongly shaped by our image of the rational being. A being who knows precisely what he or she must do with the information available in order to achieve the best possible and most efficient results, thereby maximizing their own interests. In short, a perfect information processing machine. This means that we evaluate negotiations – and human behaviour in general – from the ideal perspective of man as a rational entity. However, we now know that human capacities are more limited than this and that our view of man as a creature of reason is no longer fully valid.

Scientists and academics who study negotiations have been interested in this problem for quite some time. As early as 1982, Howard Raiffa published an influential book on negotiation in which he made a sharper distinction between *prescriptive* and a *descriptive* approach (4). The prescriptive approach focuses on the way negotiators should behave. The descriptive approach concentrates on the way negotiators actually do behave – and the mistakes they make. It is this latter approach that we will now use to gain deeper insights into the manner in which human failings can lead to the failure of negotiations.

In recent decades this descriptive approach has become more sophisticated in its analysis of the way in which negotiators deviate from rational decisions and why they do this. These deviations are influenced by biases (prejudices on which we base the majority of our evaluations) and heuristics (rules of thumb which we use to quickly give structure to our thoughts). A better understanding of biases and heuristics allow us to become more aware of the kinds of cognitive errors that we are likely to make. Errors which make it so difficult to form an accurate picture of what the other parties in the negotiating process actually want.

WHAT I REMEMBER IS IMPORTANT – ISN'T IT?

When you are taking decisions, you often attach greater weight to some pieces of information and less weight to other pieces. Sometimes this might be because the information is obviously more relevant to the decision you need to make. On other occasions, however, you might have no clear idea why you chose *this* information rather than *that* information. Research suggests that the information you use is often the information that you can remember the easiest. This easy-to-retrieve information therefore has the greatest influence on your decision-making. Even though you cannot objectively explain why this information is more important, your reasoning says: 'If I can remember it so well, it must be important.' If you have ever experienced this feeling, you are already familiar with the availability heuristic.

This heuristic relates to the spontaneous tendency of people to regard information that they can recall easily as being more valuable and more important (29). The use of this heuristic means that we are slower to use other types of information – even though these can be just as important. In other words, just because your memory is playing tricks on you, you ignore possibly vital information! This cognitive error influences your predictions to a considerable degree and can lead you to assess a situation incorrectly. Ask yourself the following question: do more people die in air accidents or in road accidents? Many people are inclined to answer 'air accidents'. Why? Because of the number of deaths which air accidents claim on a single occasion, they are always major news and offer more powerful images. For this reason, they remain longer in our memory and encourage us to overestimate the number of air deaths. In reality the number of road deaths is significantly higher. It is just that we know less about them and so they have less of an impact (30).

The overestimation of frequency of vivid and easily recalled information would not be a problem if it did not affect subsequent judgement. But it does!

A study by Robert Reyes, Bill Thompson and Gordon Bower illustrates this very clearly (31). Student participants in their study were asked to take the role of mock juries and were presented with written material on the following case. A driver had run a stop sign when driving home after a Christmas party and collided with a garbage truck. The defendant's blood alcohol had not been tested at the time and he was now being tried on the basis of circumstantial evidence. The defence was arguing that he was not legally drunk at the time of the accident.

Participants were presented with nine statements from the prosecution and nine from the defence. Each statement was one piece of evidence supporting or refuting the point that the defendant was drunk. The statements were either vivid or placid.

An example of a pallid version of the prosecution's argument was:

> On his way out of the door, Sanders staggered against a serving table, knocking a bowl to the floor.

The vivid version of the same piece of information was:

> On his way out of the door, Sanders staggered against a serving table, knocking a bowl of guacamole dip to the floor and splattering guacamole on the shag carpet.

Similarly, a pallid argument for the defence:

The owner of the garbage truck admitted under cross-examination that his garbage truck is difficult to see at night, as it is grey in colour.

And the vivid argument:

The owner said his trucks are grey, 'because it hides the dirt', and he said, 'What do you want, I should paint them pink?'

Half the students were given vivid prosecution and pallid defence statements and the other half were given pallid prosecution and vivid defence statements. As expected, more students exposed to vivid prosecution statements found the defendant to be guilty of drunk driving. This was true only when the judgements were made after a delay of 48 hours. In cases where judgements were made immediately after the presentation of evidence no such effects were found for vividness. This supports the notion that vividness enhances recall of information and this recalled information is used extensively to form judgements.

Vivid information is overweighted in judgements that are made after a delay in the presentation of information. The availability heuristic also leads to the problem that we do not consider issues that are not represented in our analysis. For example, when diagnosing cause of a problem using probability trees – a tool used by experts to ensure that they have considered all of the possibilities when assessing the probability of an event's occurring – we overweight causes that we have identified.

Baruch Fischhoff and his colleagues presented the following options to a group of mechanics to diagnose the cause for why a car will not start (32). Each of the problems was further subdivided. For example, battery charge too low was subdivided to 'faulty ground connections', 'terminals loose or corroded', and 'battery weak'. They asked the mechanics to come up with probability estimates for the major branches.

Battery charge too low	Starting system defective	Fuel system defective	Ignition system defective	Other engine problems	Vandalism	All other problems

The mechanics assigned a mean probability estimate of 0.078 to the 'all other problems' category. A similar group of mechanics was given a truncated tree, without the starting and ignition system. The earlier group had assigned mean probabilities of 0.195 and 0.144 to these branches. Rationally (and if the estimates were accurate and complete), these probabilities should go into the all other problem category and the probability of that category should increase to 0.468. The actual mean probability assigned to the all other problems category was 0.140, a slight increase but not big enough.

PEOPLE TEND TO UNDERESTIMATE THE PROBABILITY OF ALL OTHER PROBLEMS

This bias literally blinds you to the presence of the 'right' information. This can be a major problem for a negotiator, since negotiations involve the constant exchange of information. As a negotiator, it is part of your task to prepare yourself as thoroughly as possible, which means that every piece of information is potentially important. This in turn means that you need to look at every piece of information in the same way and in the same impartial light. However, this is easier said than done – and it is all the fault of the availability heuristic. The heuristic encourages us to use the information that we can remember easily as the basis for our decisions. This need not necessarily be a problem in all circumstances. But it is a problem if you are trying to evaluate a negotiating situation and are basing your decisions on this evaluation (33). By ignoring crucial information simply because it does not spring instantly to mind, you may inadvertently push the negotiations in the wrong direction. It is therefore crucial to realize that your own negotiating strategy can be influenced by the availability heuristic. Consequently, you must make a conscious effort to resist the tendency to rely only on information that your memory can recall easily.

Of course, it is not just your decisions that are influenced in this manner. Your negotiating partners will be struggling with exactly the same problem. As a strategic negotiator, it is therefore another of your tasks to try and turn the workings of availability heuristic to your advantage. Two different negotiating tactics are based on this heuristic. First of all, try to ensure that the other party remembers some things better than others; in other words, the things you want him or her to remember. You can achieve this by manipulating the order in which the different subjects are discussed. The matters that are discussed first are the matters that will remain longest in the memory. Second, you can also arrange that the information you want the other party to remember is presented in a strikingly 'memorable' way. For example, a dramatic visual presentation or a graphically detailed description can both help in this respect. Details are crucial: they make your information more dynamic and more vivid. The other party will reason that the subjects which you describe in this manner must be really important. In contrast, the information which you want the other party to forget should be described as neutrally as possible, with a complete absence of emotion and crucial detail.

VALUING WHAT WE HAVE MORE THAN WE SHOULD

It is a well-known fact: people are reluctant to throw away their old things. This is something we all discover every time we need to move house! Perhaps this is finally the moment to get rid of all that rubbish you have been keeping for years. No such luck! You may manage to part with one or two items, but most of it comes with you to your new home. There is often a similar process at work in negotiating situations. Negotiators are reluctant to let go of the certainties that they have built up in the past, even though new – and potentially more beneficial – options are now available. This can have an effect on the exchange mechanisms which are inherent to negotiations. Negotiation is essentially a matter of give and take. And as far as giving is concerned, there is usually a price tag attached. We do not like to give away the things that we regard as 'acquired rights', the possessions and certainties with which we are comfortable and familiar. And if we do give away such things, we expect a high price in return. These excessive demands are often the reason why so many negotiations run into difficulty.

People do not like change. We fear uncertainty and are inclined to hang on to existing situations as long as possible. This tendency is known as the *status quo bias* (34). If we, nevertheless, agree to change a given situation by giving up one of our acquired rights, we expect the other party to pay heavily for this 'sacrifice'. We regard the things that we have – even if we acquired them in an arbitrary fashion – as being more valuable than a truly objective assessment would suggest. Studies have shown that people will ask more money for a coffee mug that they own than for the same mug in the shops! This is a wholly irrational reflex. The overvaluing of your own property in this manner is referred to as the *endowment effect* (35). It is important to realize that this effect applies not only to material objects, but also to non-material items, such as ideas and the use of particular arguments (36). This means that negotiations will run less smoothly if the negotiators regard the subjects under discussion as their own property. Nor are such matters confined to financial and economic affairs: symbolic acquisitions from the past are also strongly affected by this proprietary approach. In particular, concessions which have been negotiated with the other party in previous negotiations are viewed as valuable possessions which are difficult to renegotiate. Feelings of this kind inevitably push up the price of the current negotiations, which increases the likelihood of stalemate.

Because of the potential difficulties which these biases can create, it is important that the negotiation process contains the possibility to appeal to some other – and impartial – third party. This third party can be used to make a more realistic assessment of the value of both sides' 'property'. Obviously, it is crucial that this intermediary should be regarded as legitimate and neutral by all the negotiating partners. At the same time, it is vital that these partners should be aware that the basing of their strategy on so-called 'acquired rights' can only have a damaging effect on the negotiations as a whole, since it will unconsciously bring all these harmful biases into play.

OVERCONFIDENCE

Most negotiators will be familiar with the following saying: 'There are no easy games.' This means that you need to approach each negotiation with the utmost professionalism and must never assume that it will be a simple matter to reach a successful final deal. Despite this, there are many negotiators who prepare in a manner that is anything but professional. Take the David Cameron example we began this chapter with. He appeared to have underestimated the difficulty and complexity of the negotiations. Is this a conscious error? Or are there other factors at play?

People have an urgent need to present themselves to the outside world in a positive light (37). For this reason, we tend to interpret the information available to us in a manner that is most advantageous to the image we wish to project. Failures will be attributed to 'unforeseen circumstances', whereas successes will be the result of our own skill and talent. In similar fashion, we interpret available information in the manner that best supports our arguments. This tendency to look at everything through rose-coloured spectacles is known as the *self-serving bias*. This bias has a huge influence on the decisions taken by negotiators. First, it means that negotiators assess themselves as 'better than average' for a wide range of negotiating qualities. For example, research revealed that 68% of American MBA students predicted that their future deals in a negotiation exercise would be amongst the best 25% of all the deals concluded (38). From a statistical point of view, this is clearly impossible! But it illustrates perfectly the irrational tendency of many negotiators, who believe that their abilities are superior to those of their rivals.

The consequences of this behaviour are alas predictable. Most negotiators run the risk of overestimating their own capabilities and are far too optimistic about their chances of success. Studies have abundantly confirmed this conclusion: if negotiators are motivated for whatever reason to present themselves in an excessively positive light, they will also overestimate the value of the deals that they are able to conclude (39, 40). In one sense, this is understandable. If you believe that you are better than your fellow negotiators, then it is logical to assume that your deals will also be better. But what if you misjudge your own abilities?

This tendency towards excessive optimism can largely be explained by the fact that people consistently overestimate the extent to which they are able to control any given situation (41). Studies have shown that two people who are required to take a decision at the same time in the 'prisoner's dilemma' game behave as though their decision will automatically influence the decision of the other player (42, 43). This is impossible, of course, since the decisions are being taken at precisely the same moment! In a negotiating context, this means that some negotiators might display cooperative behaviour because they are convinced that this will motivate the other party to cooperate as well. But if the other party decides not to cooperate, this overestimation of your own ability to control the situation may lead you to suffer unexpected losses. To avoid this possibility, it is important that negotiators should be aware of the human tendency to overestimate one's own abilities.

In other words, the self-serving bias means that there are a whole host of things that you simply do not see. The overestimation of your own skills may lead you to overlook important information or damage relations with influential contacts. This means that you might also be excluded from key coalitions, without ever realizing why. For this reason, it is essential at all stages of the negotiations to maintain an assessment of your own qualities and possibilities that is as accurate and as realistic as possible. One way to ensure this is to regularly ask the opinion of others in whose judgement you trust.

As our insight into these automatic processes gradually becomes better, it should be possible to reduce their impact on our behaviour. For example, we already know that what people regard as honest is often defined by their reflections about the reference point that is most advantageous for their own interests (44). Reflection processes of this kind are very susceptible to the influence of human biases. This is particularly true if decisions need to be made quickly or if the circumstances are ambiguous. Ambiguity simply encourages us to rely more heavily on the 'judgement' of our heuristics. This means that our evaluations and our preferences will be coloured by our own implicit self-interest. And as far as honesty is concerned, it is very easy to create this kind of ambiguity. What is honest for one party is not necessarily honest for another party, simply because they are both using different reference points. Depending upon the reference point which you use to compare the benefits you obtain from the negotiations, a deal can be seen as either honest or dishonest. As a result, one of the main problems for a negotiator is that he or she does not always know which reference point the other party is using. This information, if available, would make it much easier to understand the behaviour and attitude of the other side, which in turn would help to avoid possible escalations. Consequently, it is the task of a good negotiator to do all he or she can to reduce or eliminate the level of ambiguity in the discussions. Less ambiguity means less reflection and ensures that our biases are kept better in check during the negotiation process.

It is even possible to go further and argue that the avoidance of these biases is the moral responsibility of every negotiator. This leads us to other questions. What role do ethics play in negotiations? How much importance do we attach to morality in our decision-making? As is so often the case, there are two ways of looking at these issues. One school of thought regards deceit and manipulation as an essential part of negotiation. The other school of thought disapproves strongly of such tactics (45–47). Notwithstanding these differing viewpoints, there is, nonetheless, a consensus that negotiators should try to make use of objective moral standards. These are generally accepted principles which make clear when a negotiator has overstepped the line between honesty and dishonesty. Regrettably, the insights we possess about the ways in which people decide on such matters make the setting of these moral standards a very difficult task. Because of the implicit influence exercised by each party's own self-interest, they will often find it impossible to agree a mutually acceptable definition of such standards. Trying to impose your own views on the other side will only lead to conflict. For this reason, it is justifiable to limit ourselves to the contention that the moral responsibility of each negotiator consists of (a) a proper understanding of the cognitive errors which he or she is likely to make; (b) the realization that the other party will be affected by the same errors; and (c) the creation of circumstances which can minimize the influence of these biases on the negotiating process as a whole.

ESCALATION

Let's begin with a simple question. Have you ever stood waiting for ages for a bus, even after you realize that it is never going to come? For most people, the answer to this question is 'yes'. But why do we keep on waiting when we know that there is no point? This determination to cling to the choice we have made, even though it cannot possibly do us any good, can have far-reaching consequences. In our example with the bus, you will have wasted valuable time that you could have used on something far more useful or interesting. Yet while the moral of this story may seem obvious, it is amazing how often people are still inclined to invest their time and effort in causes which they know to be lost and which can no longer be of benefit to them. Negotiations can also escalate – or rather, deteriorate – in this manner. It sometimes happens that poor decisions are taken at the beginning of the negotiating process, which then effectively 'poison' all further discussions. The negotiators continue trying to make something of these bad decisions, but they are fighting a losing battle. Stalemate inevitably results. Once they have started on their chosen path, it is almost as if they are incapable of turning back. This phenomenon of continuing to invest in actions that can no longer yield a positive result is known as *escalation of commitment* (48).

In your role as a negotiator, it is possible that at the end of the negotiations you might come to the conclusion that you have been pursuing an impossible deal. In fact, you may even conclude that the scenario you had envisaged was doomed almost from the start. So why did you keep on investing in these negotiations? Why did you put so much time, effort and financial resources into a situation that was obviously escalating out of control? A rational approach should have told you to pull out as soon as it became clear that there was nothing to gain. Unfortunately, people in these circumstances do not always behave rationally. They develop a kind of emotional commitment towards the situation. Add to this the fact that they have already committed considerable resources, and it sometimes seems easier and better to keep going rather than pulling the plug. The explanation for this illogical behaviour is perfectly simple: people are emotionally incapable of letting go the investment they have already made (49). This persuades you to press on – and incur yet greater losses – with a cause that is already lost. We refuse to step away from the negotiating table because we are unwilling to write off the time, energy, and money that we have already spent. This, too, is illogical: our time, effort, and money are gone for good, no matter what happens! It is therefore important to find a way that allows us to cut ourselves loose from these investments emotionally. To begin with, you need to realize that the costs you have incurred in the past are irrelevant in comparison with the costs that you might still incur in the future. You should also be aware that escalation of this kind is more common in competitive negotiations, where people are more influenced by the need to protect their own reputations. Such people have a tendency to justify their actions to the outside world. This means that they have a compulsion to defend their decisions – even the bad ones. And what better way to show that you believe in your own choices than to persist with them to the bitter end – even if they bring you nothing but disappointment?

So how can we deal with this situation? What steps can a negotiator take to prevent or limit this kind of escalation?

- *Know your limits.* Make clear in advance precisely how much time and other resources you are prepared to invest in the negotiation. Set down clearly on paper the maximum limit of your investment and stick to it. This can be a very useful guideline.
- *Make sure you have alternatives.* You will be less inclined to invest in negotiations which are obviously failing if you know that you have a viable alternative, such as other potential partners to talk to. Alternative options always increase the strength of your negotiating position and protect you from escalation.
- *Take time to reflect.* Never let yourself be rushed into anything hasty! If you let your emotions get out of control, there is an increased risk that you will continue to make fruitless investments.
- *Put proper procedures in place.* Make clear arrangements about how decisions will be taken. In this way, you will be less likely to make reckless

investments. The manner in which you negotiate and the decision-making processes you employ will help you to make more balanced choices.

'WILL YOU OR SHOULD I?' THE IMPORTANCE OF ANCHORS

Which of the parties should start the negotiations? Who should be first to lay an offer on the table? This is an important question, for which many negotiators have no clear answer. Is it better to get things moving yourself? Or is it wiser to wait and see what the other side have got up their sleeve? These are matters which create uncertainty in negotiating circles. On the one hand, it can sometimes seem more advantageous to go first. At this stage, you probably still don't know what the other party really wants and this makes it difficult to assess the value of his or her initial offer. On the other hand, it might be better to bide your time and then react to this initial offer. This offer may give you plenty of new information which will allow you to better interpret the other side's objectives and intentions. In other words, there seem advantages to both strategies. So which do you choose? The results of research are clear on this point: it is generally more beneficial to be the first person to make an offer. The party who starts the negotiations frequently ends up with the best final results (8). But why?

The party who makes the first offer sets the negotiating standard for what is reasonable and what is not. Studies show that our evaluations and decisions are strongly influenced by the reference points we use, even if these reference points are sometimes arbitrary. For example, if you first give a person an arbitrary figure and then ask them to estimate the length of a particular river, they will often use this figure as their reference point. Even though this figure has nothing to do with the river in question, it exercises a strong influence on the way they look at it! In negotiations, the first offer can also be a reference point of this kind. In the professional literature this is referred to as an *anchor*. The first offer is an anchor point because the further unfolding of the negotiations are anchored (as it were) to this initial opening bid. Our subsequent definition of what we regard as a reasonable offer is anchored to the standards set by this first offer. This process also determines the negotiating room available to the different parties. And remember, as the above-mentioned studies have shown, anchor points do not necessarily have to be directly related to the negotiations themselves. A comment that you make or a statistic that you mention may be enough to move the discussions in a particular direction. The reason for the strength of this effect is to be found in the way it negatively influences the mental flexibility of the negotiator. The presence of an anchor point means that less attention is paid to other possible alternatives. Other sources of information which may have been useful for the negotiations are therefore overlooked.

Experts are also affected by anchors as a wonderful study by Greg Northcraft and Maggie Neale shows (50). In their study they had participants (48 business school undergraduates and 21 real estate agents) visit a property in Tucson, Arizona, where they were each given a ten-page packet including the following:

- Instructions
- The MLS listing sheet

- Sale information from the last six months
- Current listings in the area and the accompanying MLS listing information
- A post-view questionnaire asking them to
  - appraise the house's value;
  - set an appropriate selling price;
  - estimate an actual, reasonable sale price;
  - decide on the lowest price the house should go for.

The actual listing price and appraised value of the house was $74,900. One group's (the low price) packet had the price listed as $65,900 (which was 12% lower than the appraised value). Another group's (moderately low price) was $71,900 (4% less than the appraised value). A third group's (moderately high price) was listed at $77,900 (4% higher) and the final group (high price) had a listed price of $83,900 (12% higher). The undergraduate business students presented with the low list price appraised the value of the house as $63,571 and thought that the lowest acceptable price was $62,571; for the high list price group the two numbers were $72,196 and $69,785. Experienced realtors obtained remarkably similar results; $67,811 and $65,000 were apprised and lowest acceptable offers for realtors given low list prices and $75,190 and $72,590 were the comparable numbers for those given the high listed prices.

Note that the house was exactly the same for all the groups. And that the realtors were no less susceptible to the anchoring effect of the list price than students. Students were, however, better in one respect; 56% of them reported being influenced by the listing price while only 24% of the agents said that they had been affected by the house's list price!

The fixing of an anchor is therefore an important and potentially dangerous weapon in the hands of a negotiator. Consequently, it is vital to know exactly *when* and *how* you should use this strategy. It is always advisable to make the first offer if you are certain that you have more relevant information at your disposal than the other side. Because you know more, you are better able to assess the advantages and disadvantages of your offer. This puts you in an ideal position to influence the other party with regard to the price they must pay or the concessions they must make. If the situation is reversed, so you think that the other party has more information than you do, then it is probably wiser not to make the first offer. Wait and see what the other party has to offer: at the very least, this can win you time to gather more information about his or her aims and intention.

When you are making the first offer, it is important to be sufficiently assertive. This means that you must aim high by setting a high asking price. This has several advantages. First and foremost, it forces the other party to fix their attention on the positive qualities of your offer. They will assume that there must be good reasons why your price is so high. An obvious conclusion is that the subject under negotiation must be very valuable.

A second advantage of high initial asking price is that it later allows you to make concessions to the other side. If the other side can be given the impression that they have 'forced' your price down, this can work to the benefit of all concerned. You get the deal you want and they get the feeling that they have not given in to your 'harsh' first demands. Of course, it goes without saying that your first offer must not be so ludicrously high as to be unrealistic. The fixing of an overly aggressive anchor will simply not be believed.

Because you will not always be in a position to make the first offer, it is necessary to know how you should deal with the anchoring strategy of the other side. First of all, it is essential that you should be aware of the impact that their anchor point can have on your behaviour. Armed with this knowledge, you can make use of the following suggestions:

- Try to consciously resist the pressure to anchor your judgements on the information that is most readily available (see also the cognitive error called the availability heuristic). You would be foolish to limit yourself to assessments based exclusively on the information provided by the other party: this can only work to your disadvantage. It is therefore vital that you should continue to seek for new information which can allow you to view the anchor point from a different perspective.
- Devote sufficient time to your preparation. Think carefully about all the different alternatives that the other party might offer. This will help you to deal with his or her actual first offer in a more abstract and controlled manner. During your preparation, it is important to realize that people have a tendency to overestimate how easily they are able to deal with the pressure exerted by the other side. Once you are confronted with the real negotiations, details that you have overlooked will always emerge – be ready for this and develop an appropriate reaction strategy.
- Try to develop a counteroffer in the same manner that you would have used if you had been able to make the first offer. If you make a first offer,

you make use of a particular perspective and specific information. Use this same perspective for your counteroffer. This will mean that you will be less influenced by what the other party wants and more by the things that are important to you. This tactic will mean that your counteroffer may differ considerable from the other party's first offer. To make this less obvious and less contentious, it is a good idea to use humour in your presentation. This helps to relax tension and makes 'crazy' ideas more acceptable and discussable.

THE MYTH OF THE 'FIXED PIE'

The aim of every negotiation must be to create value for each of the participating parties. This sounds fine in theory, but practice is often very different. People still have a tendency to view decisions first and foremost from their own perspective. What we have, we hold – and we don't like to give it away. Partly for this reason, negotiators often behave in a conservative manner. Unfortunately, this does little to create added value – or 'to enlarge the pie'. Rather the contrary, in fact. The attitude which seeks to preserve the *status quo* is essentially a competitive attitude. Instead of creating a win–win scenario, it concentrates on a win–lose perspective: what is good for our side must, by definition, be bad for the other side. This way of thinking gives rise to the idea of the *fixed pie* (51). This means that the negotiations are confined to the matters which are on the table: nothing more and nothing less. A situation of this kind is characterized by what is known as a *lock-in* perspective. The attention of the negotiators is focused exclusively on the division and redivision of a well-defined package of gains and losses.

This approach obviously ensures that other and potentially more lucrative alternatives are overlooked. In the long term, it leads to a negotiating style that is impoverishing rather than enriching. Negotiators who get sucked in by this myth – namely, that added value cannot be created – believe that their conservatism actually serves the general good. However, research has shown that this is not the case. By sticking exclusively to what is currently on the table, the interests of neither side are advanced! Instead, it leads to renewed investment in existing decisions that rapidly become more and more expensive. This makes it doubly difficult to withdraw from the negotiations (see the section on escalation).

Is it possible to break through this myth of a fixed pie? Yes it is – with the right approach. The most important step a negotiator can take is to view the negotiations as an integrative rather than a distributive process (see the introductory section). This means that each party must start from the perspective that more than one solution to the negotiating problem is possible. In other words, if one proposed deal fails, there are still other which can be tried – and may lead to success. This emphasizes the importance of the point we have already made: during the preparation phase, it is vital that negotiators should consider as many different scenarios as they possibly can. This allows you to switch flexibly from one perspective to another during the actual negotiations, which will help you to keep the discussions going if things do not run smoothly at first. Finally, it also helps to adopt a more abstract way of thinking. Try to look at the long term rather than the short term. This will give you a better view of the 'big picture' and will make it easier to find the right path towards a lasting solution.

IMPATIENCE!

We are all familiar with the decisive type of person who wants to 'come to the point' straight away and who feels uncomfortable if the negotiations last longer than he or she had originally planned. However, the old saying advises us that 'patience is a virtue' – and this applies to negotiations as well. In general, people do not regard negotiations as a pleasant experience. In other words, it is an experience that you want to get behind you as soon as possible. This is hardly surprising – particularly if we remember that even in normal circumstances people have an automatic tendency to round things off quickly. Within the context of negotiations, this natural response means that many negotiators want to come to a deal with a minimum of delay – a phenomenon we refer to as *agreement bias*. However, this bias can often be fatal to the realization of your final objectives.

If you try to conclude negotiations in haste, your decisions will be even more subject to the influence of different biases. You will make greater use of heuristics, and automatic reactions will play a bigger role in your decision-making processes as the pressure of the discussions increases (the influence of system-1 thinking: see Chapter 4). In view of this, it is important to remember that it is not your task as a negotiator to bring matters to a conclusion with the greatest possible speed. If you try to do this, you will give the other party the chance to put you under increased pressure to accept their final offer.

In all negotiations, you eventually arrive at a series of breaking points – also known as deal-breakers. The deal-breakers are crucial issues which signal whether or not you are going to arrive at a deal with the other party. If you are known as a negotiator who likes to get things done quickly, this is the moment when an attentive opponent will shove a nice, big, juicy deal-breaker under your nose. If you continue to 'follow your instincts' – which will increase the influence of biases – you will most probably accept this offer. For this reason, it is again advisable to spread these breaking point moments over a longer period of time. So when the deal-breaker offer is made, ask for a further meeting at a later date. This will give you time to re-examine and re-evaluate the offer from different perspectives (system-2 thinking: see Chapter 4).

If you do decide to accept the deal-breaker, it is important to realize that this will do nothing to enhance your reputation as a negotiator. No negotiator wants to be known as 'a fast Eddy', a person who rushes through his or her deals too quickly. The outside world will view this as a lack of professionalism and an unwillingness to take responsibility. As a result, you will have more difficulties in your future negotiations. You will be less able to put others under pressure, since everyone knows that all they have to do is to wait. In short, your threats will carry no punch. It is a vicious circle from which there is no escape.

CHAPTER 4

EMOTIONS AND INTUITION

In a paper published in 2010 in the journal *Psychological Science*, Hajo Adam, Aiwa Shirako, and William Maddux provide an example of the counterproductive use of emotions in negotiations (52). The negotiations they describe related to the trade deficit talks that President Bill Clinton carried on with Japan. Determined to reduce the deficit of almost $60 billion, the president employed a particularly tough and aggressive stance in the negotiations with Japan. They say, "In one summit with Japanese Prime Minister Morihiro Hosokawa in February 1994, Clinton used some of the bluntest language by a US president with a Japanese leader to persuade Japan to open its automobile, insurance, medical-equipment, and telecommunications markets. Even though Hosokawa urged Clinton to abandon threats and anger, Clinton kept up his combative tone throughout the negotiations, and hours of heated discussion ended in an impasse. Critics of Clinton's trade policy towards Japan considered the negotiations a failure. The Japanese openly disapproved of Clinton's confrontational approach and subsequently responded with only grudging minimal concessions."

By their very nature, negotiations are situations in which emotions play an important role. In trying to promote one's best interests but at the same time being required to come to a compromise, negotiations can set loose a wide range of emotional reactions. In truth, more often than not it is the emotions which do the real talking, rather than the objective facts. As a negotiator, it is therefore important to realize that emotions will always be present when you are trying to resolve conflicts and contradictory objectives. For this reason, you cannot shut your eyes to the influence of emotions, but should instead try to use them as part of your negotiating repertoire. This in turn means that you need to gain insights into the function of emotions and understand what might happen if you attempt to integrate emotional processes into your negotiating strategy.

The first important point is that you must not necessarily regard the use of emotions as a sign of weakness. Traditional approaches to negotiation have tended to view outbursts of emotion as a lack of professionalism on the part of the negotiator. However, this interpretation is inaccurate and out of date. Recent research has increasingly shown that emotions can have a positive effect on the negotiating process. Your task as a negotiator is to understand these effects and use them to your advantage, whenever possible. There is, of course, something slightly ironic about this approach: namely, that as negotiators we are required to look at emotions in as rational a manner as possible; that we are required to control and channel something that is essentially spontaneous and unpredictable. In order to make this 'big picture' approach feasible, it is necessary to look at the effects of emotion on the negotiating process and at the way in which the question of 'intuition versus reason' influences decision-making.

TO BE ANGRY, OR NOT TO BE ANGRY?

Negotiation inevitably means that the behaviour of the other party will arouse certain emotions in you. But the opposite is also true. Your behaviour will trigger an emotional response in the other party. Consequently, it is useful to know which emotions are most commonly in play in negotiating situations and which specific effects these emotions can create.

The emotion most frequently referred to by negotiators is *anger*. This is generally seen as a negative emotion, which you express when things are not going the way you had hoped or planned. For example, we get angry if we feel that we have been unfairly treated; if the other party has been dishonest or has insulted us in an unacceptable manner. It is a powerful emotion that can put relationships under pressure. Yet, notwithstanding, this negative reputation, it is important to be aware that anger can also have positive effects on the negotiating process. In order to understand these advantages and disadvantages, it is necessary to make a distinction between the way you react to anger and the way the other party reacts. In the professional literature, this is referred to as the distinction between the intrapersonal and interpersonal effects of anger.

Intrapersonal effects

The way you experience anger can put your strategic qualities as a negotiator under additional pressure.

68

For example, research has shown that anger makes negotiators more egotistical (53). When you are angry, you are more inclined to look at the different alternatives exclusively from your own standpoint. In other words, you are more likely to make the mistake of not putting yourself in the other person's shoes. As a result, errors of this kind in the processing of information may mean that your anger persuades you to reject proposals which – viewed objectively – were actually favourable. Moreover, because angry negotiators use their own standpoint as their reference point, they are no longer able to assess the interests of the other side with the required degree of accuracy (54). The result is that the negotiations fail to yield sufficient added value to reach a mutually acceptable solution.

Fortunately, the effects of anger are not wholly negative. If we look at the manner in which evaluations and decisions are made, it can often result in a number of advantages. Because of its strong focus on self-interest, anger can lead to arrogance, excessive self-confidence, an overestimation of your own powers and a strong reaction towards unacceptable behaviour on the part of the other party. At first glance, this might not sound all that positive. However, these same effects can work to your advantage when you need to make a decision. For example, they may help you to be more resolute, more willing to take action. You will have fewer doubts and be less afraid of taking risks. This will often allow you to make a more appropriate response to the behaviour of the other party. Bearing in mind that being overly cautious is a common weakness in negotiators, this can be of great benefit. A desire to be cautious makes it difficult to take strong decisions, and this lack of decisiveness may push the negotiations in the direction of stalemate. If you are conscious of this fact, a certain degree of anger may help you avoid the pitfalls of hesitation and indecision.

Interpersonal effects

If you are angry, this will probably not go unnoticed by the other party. But what effect will your anger have on this other party? In essence, anger is an aggressive attitude that we take towards someone else (55). However, aggression can often lead to good final results. This is primarily because the other party may feel compelled to pull back or make concessions in response to this aggression. Your anger will seldom lead to a situation where the other party is intrinsically motivated to take account of your interests; on the contrary, they will feel as though they are being forced against their will. Yet even though your anger will make the other party uncomfortable and possibly even angry in turn, it is still possible to speak of a positive effect.

Anger can also work to your advantage in negotiations between parties who do not know each other very well. This is above all the case for smaller deals. In these circumstances, anger is seen as a signal that a negotiator is not easy to confuse or knock off balance (56). In fact, his or her anger is a sign of strength and toughness (57). As a consequence, the other parties will conclude that the angry party will not make any further concession, because their anger shows that they have reached their limits. Because people are naturally reluctant to jeopardize relationships, these other parties will be more inclined to back down and make concessions of their own. In short, it does not work to your advantage to show too quickly that you are satisfied. This will make the other party more reluctant to moderate their own demands or accept yours. Anger can therefore work to your advantage as long as you use it in a manner that says something about your determination and your belief in your own abilities. In this sense, anger can enhance your reputation as a negotiator, by making clear that you are someone who knows what you want and know how to get it (see Chapter 6). Yet despite this positive message, it is, nonetheless, necessary to realize that research into these matters has shown that the 'anger effect' has its limits.

First and foremost, it is important that the other party should be able to interpret your anger in the right way, so that they can draw the right conclusions: namely, that you are a tough guy. This means that you must show your anger at the right moment and in the right manner. It is also a strategy to which you need to devote the necessary time and preparation. Studies have proven that anger is less good at forcing concessions in situations where decisions need to be taken quickly (58). If the other party is under time pressure, they will pay much less attention to your emotions. They will simply not have the time to process this information. Consequently, you must always ensure that the reason for your anger is apparent and that the message it conveys is unambiguous. And make sure that the other party notices it!

Another aspect which the angry negotiator needs to monitor is the relative distribution of power in the negotiation process (59). Being angry in a negotiating context is a very aggressive posture to adopt. If you are in a strong negotiating position, this can often work in your favour. You will 'persuade' the other party to make concessions more quickly. Even so, you must remember that these are 'forced' concessions and are therefore dependent upon the power of your position rather than the power of your argument. This can rebound against you, if you find yourself in a weaker position later on in the same negotiations or in other negotiations at a later date (the way in which you can change a weak negotiating position is discussed in Chapter 7). Similarly, anger which is expressed by a weak party will often incite the anger of the other negotiating parties. In view of the fact that these other parties occupy a higher position in the power hierarchy, there is a strong likelihood that they will make you pay for your outburst of anger at a later stage of the negotiating process. Sooner or later, the stronger parties will make their power felt and will force you to make concessions.

And finally the display of anger has different effects across cultures as our introductory example states. Eastern cultures and Japan in particular do not view the display of anger favourably. Here one needs to be very careful that the display of emotions is not viewed as inappropriate or insulting.

All the above should make it clear that it is very difficult to avoid anger in the course of your negotiations. For this reason, you must learn how to deal with this key emotion, so that your own emotional reactions do not damage your cause. As research has shown, however, this is easier said than done. Dealing with anger in a constructive manner is a major challenge. But perhaps there is another way to show your disapproval through a less disruptive negative emotion, an emotion that causes less damage and can even create positive results with minimal effort on your part.

This emotion is the emotion of disappointment. People show their disappointment if they see that the behaviour of the other party has not lived up to their expectations. The demonstration of the emotion indicates that you wish things had turned out differently. As such, it implies a request to change the existing situation for the better. Disappointment is not an aggressive emotion. In fact, it can be regarded as a form of constructive criticism. Studies confirm that the expression of disappointment arouses a far less negative reaction in the other party than the expression of anger. Even more importantly, the expression of disappointment often encourages the other party to take action to relieve your uncomfortable feeling by adopting a more cooperative attitude (60). Conclusion? There is nothing wrong with being angry, but you need to do it at the right moment and in the right way – otherwise it might come back to haunt you. In contrast, expressing disappointment can never do you any harm.

IF EMOTIONS HAVE NOTHING TO DO WITH THE NEGOTIATIONS

The role of emotions during negotiations is viewed from a perspective which says that the behaviour of the other party is responsible for what you feel. Consequently, researchers focus primarily on the specific emotions which can be aroused by the negotiating process. It almost goes without saying that it is very important to be able to identify these emotions and learn how to deal with them (61).

However, more recent studies have suggested that negotiators also need to learn how to deal with emotions that are not directly triggered by the negotiations. Why? Because emotions that have nothing to do with the actual negotiating process can still have a powerful influence of your behaviour during that process.

The emotions which we experience can remain in our system for a long time. This means that we carry certain emotions from one situation to another. These emotions are part of our so-called 'non-task communication'. This type of communication is totally separate from the objectives you are trying to achieve in the course of your negotiations and consequently is not directly relevant to the negotiation process. Even so, this communication can be an important factor in reaching a successful final agreement. Research has confirmed that emotions which you experience in contexts other than the situation in which you are currently engaged can significantly influence your levels of confidence and trust in that unrelated situation (62). The results of these studies showed that people who are angry have the greatest difficulty in giving trust to others, whereas people who are happy have much less of a problem. People who are sad are somewhere between the two. This demonstrates clearly that emotions can lead to a more or less trustful attitude in other contexts than the context where the emotion was first experienced. For a negotiator, this means that he or she needs to pay careful attention to the emotional state of the other party at the beginning of the negotiations. The type of emotions that the other party is displaying at this critical moment can have a major impact on the remainder of the negotiating process.

In order to accurately assess the presence and influence of particular emotions, it is necessary to have the right skills. An important variable which assists you to identify and process emotional data is your own emotional intelligence (63, 64). Emotional intelligence can help you to become a successful negotiator by allowing you to access and interpret the emotional signals being transmitted by the other party. The following are examples of how emotional intelligence can be used to ask and answer the right questions:

- If the emotions displayed by the other party are verbally ambiguous, you can, nonetheless, assess what he or she is feeling on the basis of their non-verbal behaviour and other outward physical changes which they cannot control. Examples of such uncontrolled responses include the movement of the Adam's apple and blushing in response to certain questions.
- If you want to ask a favour of another party (see also the strategies used to acquire power in Chapter 7), you need to assess who is the best person to ask and when is the best moment to ask. To do this, you need to have a good idea of their state of mind. Are they paying attention? Do they give the impression of wanting to move forward quickly? Or are they more interested in delay?
- Imagine that the other party receives either good news (which makes him or her happy) or bad news (that makes him or her angry) at precisely the moment when you were planning to reveal your demands. Are you able to assess whether or not you need to try and change the emotional mindset of the other party and, if so, how?

■ In the course of the negotiations you have received a number of compliments from the other party. As a result, you feel that you have the situation completely under control. Are you the type of negotiator who is still able in these circumstances to assess rationally what to do and what to demand? Or are you the type of negotiator who gets carried away in the success of the moment?

A good negotiator will recognize these situations. He or she not only knows how to deal with them correctly, but can also anticipate and exploit them. Consequently, emotional intelligence benefits not only the manner in which you negotiate and your final end result but also the manner in which you approach your preparation. In short, a successful negotiator knows not only what the other party says but also what he or she is feeling.

WHEN INTUITION TAKES OVER: SYSTEM-1 VERSUS SYSTEM-2 THINKING

Most expert negotiators would tell you that you must learn to trust you intuition. Intuition, they say, is everything! If we look at reality, however, we must conclude that intuition only works sometimes. So where does this leave us? What value must we attach to the use of intuition? To provide an answer to this question, we need to look more closely at the distinction between *system-1 thinking* and *system-2 thinking*. This distinction was made by the researchers Stanovich and West to explain why negotiators so often deviate from the rational and the logical (see Chapter 3) (65). System-1 thinking is characterized by a rapid and automatic way of thinking, which is strongly influenced by emotions. System-2 thinking is less rapid and involves conscious thought processes, which are more controlled. Both systems have their advantages and disadvantages.

For most negotiators, not every decision carries the same level of importance. For decisions which do not have major consequences or are not high on the list of the negotiator's priorities, the decisions can be taken quickly, easily and almost unconsciously (system-1 thinking). For more serious decisions, however, which have potentially important consequences and therefore represent a crucial step in the negotiations, system-2 thinking is required. Put like this, it does not seem all that difficult to determine your approach to decision-making in a systematic and controlled manner. Unfortunately, many negotiations take place in high-pressure situations. The other parties will attempt to knock you off balance, insisting you follow their line and trying to force you into quick decisions. Faced with lack of time, in these circumstances many negotiators fall back on system-1 thinking, whereas this is precisely the moment that they should be relying on system-2. In short, it is crucial that negotiators understand which system is most appropriate in any given situation. It is even more crucial that they then use the appropriate system, in order to avoid the mistake outlined above.

Researchers Max Bazerman and Deepak Malhotra have developed a number of suggestions which can help you to ensure that you use system-2 thinking whenever it is really necessary (66).

- Suggestion 1: You must know exactly what type of negotiations you are required to conduct and when. Make a list of your most important forthcoming negotiations and add an assessment of their relative importance. This can help you to decide what type of thinking is most appropriate in each case. We all have a tendency to fill our appointments book to the brim. This means that important and less important matters can follow each other in rapid succession. As a negotiator, it is vital to make a distinction between these two categories. This will not only make clear to you when you need to be aware of the possible problems of time pressure but also when you need to give your decisions more careful thought.

- Suggestion 2: Ensure that you never allow yourself to be pressurized into making quick decisions. Too many negotiators give in to this type of pressure, either from fear of losing the deal or from fear of creating a bad impression with the other party. In reality, this is really a form of imaginary pressure. No one will think badly of you if you say that you need more time to reach your decision! On the contrary, asking for more thinking time shows that you are giving serious consideration to the other party's proposal. Use this extra time to your advantage: not only to think more fully about what you want to do but also to give the other party the feeling that they are important.

- Suggestion 3: Avoid deciding everything at the same time. People have a natural desire to conclude matters as quickly as possible (see Chapters 3 and 5). In other words, you don't need the other party breathing down your neck in order to experience time pressure: it is often self-inflicted. To avoid being rushed into overhasty decisions, divide the time available for negotiation into different periods, with decisions only to be taken after the end of each period.

The idea of system-1 and system-2 thinking sounds logical. It offers a controlled approach which allows you to avoid potential pitfalls. Nevertheless, it is important not to forget that intuition is not always bad – or wrong. As we have previously mentioned, not every decision is vital. We have all experienced the manner in which most of our routine daily decisions are made on a kind of automatic pilot, and this often works extremely well. In other words, system-1 thinking is perfect for getting on with everyday life. Moreover, recent research has also shown that fast decision-making can sometimes work very well – even as well as system-2 thinking – but only in the case of certain complex decisions (67). These decisions are so complex that a thorough and controlled analysis of the situation does not produce satisfactory results.

If you see that system-1 thinking is arousing negative emotions – for example, frustration and incomprehension – you should make the switch to system-2 thinking. It is important that the decision-making process should not leave you with a bad taste in your mouth, even if the end results it achieves are good. You need to be satisfied not only with the decisions but also with the manner in which you reached those decisions. A good result with negative emotions attached is something you should try to avoid, if at all possible. This reasoning takes us to the very heart of the matter. For the decisions that really count, it is essential that you can analyse the situation in a conscious and controlled manner. But this approach must not be pushed through at the expense of your own feelings. If you notice that a rational analysis of the decision-making process is making you uncomfortable, this is the moment when you should start listening to your intuition. And the moral of this story? Know what you want to decide and why, but don't forget to be happy about it!

CHAPTER 5

THE IMPACT OF FRAMING ON NEGOTIATIONS

One of the authors was once advising a young colleague who was negotiating over the terms of their contract with the dean of the school. After a series of conversations the colleague, who was (and is) a very pleasant and engaging person, and the dean arrived at a satisfactory conclusion. The colleague then proceeded to ask us whether she should ask the dean to put down some of the agreements in writing. The author said no and pointed out that asking for a written confirmation may be tantamount to saying that they did not trust the dean to fulfil their part of the deal. It also moved the negotiation from a relational frame to a transactional one, which means that cooperation and goodwill could not be assumed anymore.

Research shows that our behaviour and the way we make decisions are strongly affected by the context in which we find ourselves. In fact, the context can have a more decisive influence on the final outcome of the negotiations than the personality of the negotiator despite our beliefs to the contrary (13). It is not only the objective context which creates this effect; even the subjective naming of that context can also play a significant role. Subtle cues in the environment can trigger a switch in behaviour such that we change from a cooperative negotiator who tries to maximize the pie for everyone to a suspicious negotiator who does not believe what the other party is saying. To be a successful negotiator, you need to acquire insights into the way in which a situation and the manner in which it is described can act on the thoughts and emotions of a human being.

SOCIAL FRAMES

Each negotiation is unique. Negotiations can differ in terms of the objectives you are seeking to reach, the information you have at your disposal, the options which you can choose, and so on. All these different elements determine the manner in which you will look at the negotiation. In psychology, the way in which we look at any given situation is known as framing. Framing refers to the mental structure which we use to make the situation in question more readily understandable and accessible. This structure – whatever it might be – is then expressed in linguistic terms. For example, some negotiators might describe a situation as 'conflict resolution' whereas other might refer to 'contractual discussions'. The difference in terminology is largely influenced by the elements which the negotiator regards as being central to the negotiations on hand. If the negotiator thinks that there are fundamental differences of opinion between the negotiating parties, he or she will be inclined to view the negotiations in terms of possible disputes: hence he or she will talk of 'conflict resolution'. If, however, he or she views the situation more as a business transaction, in which the differences of opinion will be formally resolved to the mutual benefit of all concerned, the negotiator will be more likely to refer to the negotiations as 'contractual discussions'. These different interpretations of the same situation can lead to important differences in behaviour.

The ability to recognize the framing used by the other negotiating parties is important, since it can help you better understand their actions and their words. This is particularly useful if their behaviour is significantly different from what you had expected. This can create uncertainty, and so it is necessary to check whether this uncertainty has been caused as a result of the different interpretations of the situation being used by the different parties. During political negotiations we often see that the different parties can often interpret the same situation in radically different ways. These differences in interpretation – of which the negotiators are not always aware – can also result in amazement at the behaviour of the other side. The recent coalition negotiations in Belgium have illustrated this phenomenon all too clearly. For many key issues the French- and Dutch-speaking political parties have diametrically opposed patterns of expectation, particularly with regard to what should be negotiated and how it should be negotiated. Moreover, in many countries, parties on the left of the political spectrum differ significantly from parties on the right in the extent to which they regard the negotiations as 'conflictual' or 'contractual'. The parties which view the negotiations in terms of 'contractual discussions' will assume that trust in an economic frame need not be based on respect and emotion (see Chapter 6). The parties which view the negotiations in terms of the resolution of relational disputes will continue to focus on respect and empathy for all concerned. In other words, the respective use of economic or the relational frame leads to different interpretations and expectations. As long as the parties fail to realize that it is possible to apply different frames at the same time to the same situation – and, more importantly, why people need to do this – the negotiations will quickly lead to stalemate.

Various studies have shown that the process of framing can have a significant impact on the final outcome of the negotiations (68). In an experiment, a game was given two different names. The game in question was the well-known 'prisoner's dilemma'. In this game two prisoners must decide whether or what they want to cooperate with each other. The dominant strategy is not to cooperate. If one party wants to cooperate but the other one doesn't, the party which refused to cooperate will ultimately gain the greater reward. If both parties want to cooperate, the collective interests of them both are served equally. This means that in order to maximize the gains for all concerned – which must be the objective of all negotiations – it is necessary that everyone should cooperate. However, the study showed that people were twice as likely to be cooperative when the game was called 'The Community Game' than when it was called 'The Wall Street Game' (69).

These results confirm the supposition that the way in which a particular situation is described or named can induce different behaviour. If the frame is purely economic – The Wall Street Game – negotiators will set about their task in a more calculated manner, so that the importance of interpersonal relationships will be reduced. In other words, there is greater competitiveness. If, however, the frame is given a more relational name – The Community Game – attitudes generally become more cooperative. The existence of this implicit influence makes it imperative that negotiators should pay close attention to the manner in which the negotiations are described by their other negotiating partners. This knowledge can lead to a better understanding of each other's motivation and so help to avoid stalemate situations.

NEGOTIATING GAINS AND LOSSES

The way in which the parties concerned interpret the negotiations can have major consequences for the type of behaviour that can reasonably be expected from them. In this respect, an important type of framing is the extent to which the negotiations are viewed in terms of the relative distribution of gains and losses. How far is each step in the negotiation process interpreted as a victory or a defeat? This perception of gain versus loss can significantly influence the further development of the discussions. Research indicates that people have a very different attitude, depending on whether they are faced with the prospect of gain or loss (70).

Let us return briefly to the example of a house which is on the market for 200,000 pounds. This time our buyer is only prepared to pay a maximum of 180,000 pounds. However, the seller sticks rigidly to his or her lowest limit of 185,000 pounds. This means that there is only negative room for negotiation, since the upper limit of the buyer and the lower limit of the seller are separated by a difference of 5,000 pounds. In order to solve this problem, we need to influence the perception of both parties in such a way that neither of them believes that they have made a loss. Imagine that they propose to split the difference, so that a price is fixed at 182,500 pounds. This can be viewed as either a gain or a loss. Depending on the perception adopted by the parties, the deal may go through – or it may not. The seller can see the new asking price as a further concession of 2,500 pounds (185,000 − 2,500), while the buyer may see the new price as an additional financial commitment (180,000 + 2,500). In other words, both parties view the new arrangement as a loss. If they do this, there is every chance that there will be no sale. However, it is also possible to view the new price from a 'win–win' perspective. The seller can actually regard this price as a gain of 2,500 pounds, if he or she tries to look at things from the buyer's point of view. This buyer only wanted to pay a maximum of 180,000 pounds, but has now agreed to go to 182,500: a higher amount, which can therefore be regarded as a gain of 2,500 euros for the seller. The buyer can look at things in much the same light. Originally, the seller was not prepared to accept a penny less that 185,000 pounds, but has now agreed to settle for 182,500: a lower amount than he or she wanted and therefore a gain of 2,500 pounds for the buyer, if viewed from the seller's perspective. If this more positive frame is used by both sides, it is likely that the sale will be concluded.

This example shows that looking at something in terms of gain and loss can have a serious impact on the decisions taken by negotiators. There is convincing research evidence to show that negotiators are influenced in an irrational manner in their response towards risks by either positive (gain) or negative (loss) frames (40, 71). As a result, we now know that people are more strongly motivated to avoid losses than they are to seek gains of an equal level. In other words, losses weigh more heavily than gains in the evaluation of any given situation. This means in turn that negotiators are more inclined to take risks when losses are at stake rather than gains.

This idea that losses have a greater impact on negotiating behaviour than gains has implications for a wide range of influencing strategies. Imagine that you are trying to persuade your negotiating partner to take more account of your arguments. A useful tactic in these circumstances is to lower your price; in other words, to voluntarily accept a loss. By activating this frame of loss, the other party will become more responsive to your arguments. If he or she views these arguments from a positive perspective – which is certainly how your willingness to reduce your price will be viewed – you may still be able to win the day. If, however, you wish to avoid the possibility that the other party will take more risks to push through his or her own point of view, you need to define the negotiations in terms of gain. In this way, you will be better able to prevent your opponent from becoming too competitive. Situations which involve potential loss always incite more aggressive, risky behaviour. Before the outbreak of the recent crisis, this tactic of influencing the motivation of others through the use of positive or negative framing was widely used in the financial sector. Consider the example of the manager of an international banking concern who wants to increase his or her company's profits. He or she can choose between the two motivational techniques outlined above. Technique 1 involves telling the staff that the bank is already doing well, but that in the future it can do even better (the use of the gain perspective). Technique 2 involves telling the staff that the bank is performing 2% less well than its competitors and that this situation cannot be allowed to continue (use of the loss perspective). Which option should he or she take? In this particular scenario, technique 2 was chosen: a conscious use of the loss perspective to stimulate greater risk-taking, in the hope that this would increase the chance of quick profits, was preferred.

How can we explain this effect of the different perceptions of gain and loss? With regard to gain, it is possible to speak about a continuous increase in utility. Greater gain means greater subjective value. However, this subjective value decreases proportionally as objective gain increases. In other words, your first million pounds has greater utility than each subsequent million that you earn. Or to put it another way, the value of each successive million becomes slowly less and less. Yet notwithstanding this depreciation in subjective value, you will never reach a situation of negative emotional perception. No one is ever going to refuse an extra million – no matter how many they already have! This logic has consequences for the manner in which you should share good news. It is advisable to share good news over a period of time, rather than all in one go. This allows you to accumulate the positive effect of your gain framing over a longer time span – although this, too, will be subject to a gradual diminution.

With regard to loss, we can indeed speak of negative emotional value. As we have already mentioned, people are more highly motivated by the avoidance of loss than by the possibility of gain. Consequently, each new loss – in comparison with each new gain – hits harder and harder. This means that an accumulation of losses over a period of time can weigh very heavily on a person. After all, no one wants to be an extra million pounds in debt. For this reason, it is preferable to announce bad news immediately and in full, rather than seeking to spread it out over a number of weeks, months, or even years.

CONCRETE VERSUS ABSTRACT THOUGHT

Can you be emotionally involved in the negotiations that you are required to carry out? If the things to be discussed touch you personally, is it not wiser to leave the task to someone else? These are important questions. The level of your personal commitment may have implications for the manner in which the negotiations are conducted. Numerous stories exist of negotiators who identify themselves so closely with the issues at stake that the whole negotiating process becomes a Via Dolorosa for all concerned. An important piece of negotiating wisdom recommends that you need to be able to distance yourself at regular intervals from what you are doing at the negotiating table. Even so, there are many others who contend that a high degree of passion is necessary to argue on behalf of something you believe in. If a negotiator does not live and breathe the negotiations, how can you expect him or her to fight for – let alone achieve – the final objectives? These are both valid opinions. But which one is right?

Research has indicated that the psychological distance between the actual performance and the mental performance of your actions can have a major influence on your own perceptions, motivation and behaviour. In this type of research, psychological distance is examined in terms of physical distance (being near or far away) or temporal distance (short term or long term). Being near activates a concrete way of thinking, while being far away activates an abstract way of thinking. Things which happen in the short term (a day or so later) likewise lead to a more concrete method of evaluation, whereas things which happen in the long term (a year or so later) lead to a more abstract way of thinking. This means that the shorter the psychological distance, the more concrete your approach is likely to be. As a result, you will focus more closely on details. A greater psychological distance implies a more abstract overall approach, but this will allow you to see things more in perspective.

Studies have proven that these mindsets can be very relevant for the decisions which you need to take during negotiations. We know, for example, that if people think in an abstract manner, they are more likely to uphold general moral standards. This will encourage them to take more moral decisions than people who think in a more concrete manner (72). The same studies also show that a more abstract way of thinking also results in a greater degree of self-control (73): you will think abstractly, you will be less inclined to accept an immediate (and usually smaller) reward, but will look for a reward over a longer period (which will usually be much bigger). People who think concretely prefer to take the money and run – or 'go for the quick buck', as it is sometimes known. Finally, the research data suggest that in general abstract thinking helps to make the negotiations run more smoothly (74). This makes it easier to reach a final solution that is acceptable to all concerned, which is not always possible with a more opportunistic concrete approach.

These studies suggest that it is very important not to become too bogged down in the details of your negotiations. This can lead to less than optimal results.

Fortunately, there are a number of tricks which can help to ensure that you use a more abstract mindset when you are performing your negotiating tasks. For each decision that you are required to take, try to imagine that its effects will only be felt in the long term and that the other party is located in some far-away place. There is copious evidence to show that this approach to decision-making activates a more abstract way of thinking. And given the fact that abstract thought processes seem to offer a number of potential advantages, it is well worth taking a little time to prepare and perform this mental exercise!

SOCIAL PRESSURE!

Before you actually start the negotiations, it is advisable to communicate clearly about the manner in which you intend to negotiate. Information about the values and norms which you are planning to use will ensure that people will understand what is acceptable for you and what is not. Most of us are happy to be guided by these social conventions. We do not like to stray too far from what the majority says and does. This is known as the conformist tendency: our desire to 'follow the crowd' (75–77). The negotiating party that is able to set their norms first will therefore have considerable influence on the further development of the negotiating process. They set the tone for the values which will be regarded as important during all subsequent discussions. In short, they define what is right and what is wrong; what can and cannot. This is a huge advantage. If you want to make your value framework the dominant value framework, it is crucial to obtain the support of the majority as quickly as possible. This implies the need to create a coalition which is strong enough to exclude any other parties who fail to abide by the agreed social norms – even if this exclusion is limited to social exclusion through stigmatization.

It regularly happens during negotiations that one of the parties is given a good dressing-down by some or all of the others, simply because they failed to follow the rules. But what are these rules, exactly? And who sets them? If we are talking about power politics, then the rules are obviously the rules which the strongest power bloc imposes on its weaker partners. In reality, however, a dressing-down in these circumstances is more a matter of 'the pot calling the kettle black'. One of the parties is given a ticking off because it seemingly fails to comply with the agreed social norms. But these social norms have been defined by the dominant coalition with the specific purpose of influencing and even directing the behaviour of the other negotiating parties! This smacks of hypocrisy rather than moral rectitude.

Be that as it may, negotiations are continually subject to all different types of social pressure. Sometimes this pressure is explicit, but more often it is active behind the scenes. As a result, it is not always easy to identify the social influencing strategies being used by the other side. And if you can identify them, it is difficult to resist them. One of the most well-known techniques of this kind is the so-called 'good cop–bad cop' routine. In this technique, two different parties attempt to influence your perception of reality by adopting radically divergent forms of behaviour. The first of the two parties puts forward a worst-case scenario, which is designed to temper your expectations. However, this party is often so extreme that no one is prepared to do business with him or her. This is the 'bad cop': his or her proposals are simply unacceptable. At this point, the second party – the 'good cop' – enters the scene. He or she attempts to neutralize the bad cop by putting forward a better proposal: not necessarily the proposal you were hoping for, but certainly better than anything on offer from the bad cop.

The result is that many people are now prepared to accept the proposal made by the good cop – even though they would probably never have accepted this same proposal if it had not been preceded by the even worse proposal of the bad cop! How does this work? Simple enough – when you know how. The bad cop has set down a marking point which strongly influences the manner in which the proposals of all other parties will be evaluated. However, this marking point has created such a low level of expectation that the new proposal made by the good cop does not need to be significantly better in order to be accepted. It is a bit better – and that is the important thing. This allows (in relative terms) a 'good' relationship to be built up with the good cop, as opposed to the obviously 'bad' relationship with the bad cop. Moreover, by his or her apparently supportive behaviour, the good cop confirms your opinion that the bad cop's behaviour was unacceptable – and so the trap is closed.

This all sounds fairly simple, but the tactic can actually be quite hard to identify – especially if you are dealing with talented actors. Often you only realize what is going on after you have already gone too far to turn back! Once the bad cop has been able to implant his or her marking point into your head, it is difficult to escape from the influence of his or her frame of reference. Unconsciously, your way of thinking is 'infected' by his or her way of thinking – and this colours every decision you make (see Chapters 3 and 5). When the penny finally does drop, it is important that you should make clear to both the good cop and the bad cop that you know exactly what they are trying to do. After that, you should only rely on objective facts, and not on the 'reconstituted' facts specially prepared for you by this untrustworthy double act and their marking point. However, be careful not to create the impression that you are deliberately blowing up the negotiations. Make clear that you are willing to continue discussions, but try to establish a new marking point based on objective criteria as quickly as possible. It may even be worthwhile attempting to split up the good cop–bad cop partnership by only agreeing to talk further with the bad cop. This will allow you to neutralize the original bad offer and will make it possible to restart negotiations with a clean slate – and without the pressure of a second party breathing down your neck.

WHERE DO WE NEGOTIATE?

'Your place or mine?' This is not normally a question that you would associate with negotiations! Even so, it is highly relevant. Where are you going to conduct your negotiations? This may seem almost a banal consideration, when you have so many other weightier negotiating matters on your mind. But is it? If you were a sportsman, the answer would be easy: you would want to play 'at home'. This would allow you to draw inspiration from the encouragement of your own supporters. But negotiations do not take place in public arenas. So is there still such a thing as 'home advantage' in the negotiating world?

It cannot be denied that there are numerous practical advantages to conducting negotiations in familiar surroundings. You lose less time because there is less need to travel. You know the location well and feel comfortable in it. In short, even negotiators, it seems, prefer to play at home rather than away. And research has confirmed the benefits of this approach: negotiators consistently achieve better results if they are operating close to their home base. The reverse is also true: negotiators who are forced to work away from their home environment perform less well. Part of the reason for this is that the home player has more self-confidence, inspired by the familiarity of the setting. As a result, the visiting negotiators need to develop mechanisms during their preparation period which can boost their own self-confidence (78).

This suggests that there is a good deal of truth to the commonly held assumption that negotiating 'on your own patch' is better than negotiating on 'foreign soil'. But is this always the case? Some people have suggested that negotiating in a location chosen by the other side can also have its benefits. In particular, it can help to create goodwill. However, practice has shown that this is only the case if there is a large difference in the relative strengths of the negotiating partners. If you are clearly the superior power, you will obviously be in a position to make small concessions to the other side. Agreeing to their suggested location might be one such small concession. If you are clearly the weaker power, you may hope to whip up some sympathy for your cause by agreeing to meet 'in the lion's den'.

Notwithstanding the popular belief that you should not lightly surrender home advantage, there are nonetheless a number of less positive matters which you should not overlook:

- Negotiating in familiar surroundings may be more comfortable, but this very comfort may take the edge off your preparations. Because you have no need to travel, you tend to overestimate the time at your disposal to make all the necessary arrangements. Remember, however, that there are always more interruptions and distractions at your home base than elsewhere: the phone keeps on ringing and people keep on calling in to your office. In contrast, the visiting negotiators have a long journey in which they can discuss their approach to the negotiations undisturbed.
- As the home party, you are also obliged to make all the practical arrangements for the negotiations. This is an added impingement on your time – but does not affect the visitors.
- If you find it necessary to break off the negotiations as the home party, this effectively means that you need to show the other side of the door. There is no symbolic way of leaving this (real or metaphorical) door ajar, in the hope that they might reconsider their position. If you ask someone to leave your office (or conference centre, or country), the breach will usually be final.
- As the visiting party, it is easier for you to delay or spin out the negotiations, because you are operating in 'foreign' surroundings where you do not always have the necessary information to hand. This is a useful tactic which is not available to the home negotiators. It allows the visitors to play for time or

to avoid being rushed into hasty decisions without proper consideration.

IF REPRESENTATIVES ARE CONDUCTING THE NEGOTIATIONS

It is a simple physical fact of life: if you are the head of a large company or political party, it is impossible for you to be everywhere at the same time. As a result, negotiations in your name will frequently be conducted by your representatives. In this context, we therefore need to ask whether negotiation through intermediaries – particularly if more than one intermediary is involved – does not make the negotiating situation more complex and more uncertain than is really necessary, because research has shown that this type of negotiation has both clear advantages and disadvantages.

Representatives find themselves in a position to negotiate because they have been delegated to do so by their business or political leaders. However, delegation can lead to problems if the negotiations are being conducted with a view to dividing up the benefits of a positive final settlement. For example, studies suggest that the role played by a representative can be very influential in cases where it is necessary to share money with another party. Representatives who are required to share behave less cooperatively than people who are sharing in their own right. In particular, representatives feel less constrained to ensure a fair distribution of the available cash. As a consequence, they are more inclined to behave competitively. It is almost as if the delegation of a task absolves them from all responsibility: 'I am only doing this for the boss, and so the responsibility is his and not mine; consequently, there is no need for me to behave fairly.' These findings make clear that you need to be extra careful if you know that your negotiating partner is acting as a representative for someone in authority over him or her. You can be reasonably sure that this person will approach his or her task aggressively and competitively.

Negotiating with a representative is inevitably a complex business. You are not negotiating directly with the person who has the power to make the final decisions. On the contrary, you are obliged to deal with his or her 'front man'. This front man will not only feel a lesser sense of responsibility than the master but will also be more likely to renege on any agreements he or she makes. This type of behaviour might result in you being unconsciously manipulated to tie yourself to the suggestions of the other party. This is illustrated by the principle of the representative as the 'hidden cop'.

Imagine that you want to buy a car. You pay a visit to your favourite dealer and you are immediately approached by a salesperson. You tell him or her about your wishes and preferences. He or she seems to understand your needs and gives you a full guided tour of the premises. You are impressed with what he or she shows you and so you decide to open negotiations for a possible purchase. The salesperson senses that you are prepared to pay good money to get something you really like and so he or she suggests a wide range of options. However, his or her sales pitch is not always clear; on some points he or she remains fairly vague. These points, he or she tells you, need to be decided by the boss. Unfortunately, the boss is not in the garage that day, but the salesperson assures you that there will be no problems...This is when the warning lights should start flashing. On no account should you be tempted to proceed further; instead, you should tell the salesperson politely but firmly that you want to continue your negotiations directly with the person who has the power to make the decisions.

But what if you ignore the warning lights? What if you *are* tempted to proceed further? Firstly, the salesperson will attempt to find the limits of your negotiating room. In other words, he or she will try to get the most out of the deal – for himself or herself. If you agree to the terms of this deal, the salesperson will still need to contact his or her boss: after all, he or she is the only person who can draw up and approve the necessary papers. But by now you are hooked. You want that car so badly that you dare not imagine that things could still go wrong at this late stage. Unfortunately, they can. The boss now tells you that the salesperson has made a mistake: you cannot possibly have such a magnificent car and all the options for the price he or she quoted. If you still want to go ahead, it will now cost you considerably more. Of course you still want to go ahead! You can already see yourself cruising around town to the envious glances of all your friends and acquaintances. And to convince yourself, you will start finding benefits in this wonder car that no one else has even mentioned. It is no longer just the price that is important, but also the beautiful upholstery and the driving comfort: for this kind of luxury you must expect to pay a little bit more...

And the moral of this story? Namely, that you should consider skipping the phase with the representative and move on quickly to direct negotiations with the person who is in a position to decide what is possible and what is not. You want to talk to the organ grinder – not his or her monkey! But if you do find yourself unavoidably embroiled with representatives, delegates, salespersons, and the like, prepare yourself for the worst. Use of dishonest procedures and failure to honour their agreements will be part of the course until the man with the real power finally shows up on the scene.

CHAPTER 6

TRUST AND DISTRUST

The relationships between the negotiating parties play a major role in negotiation outcomes (45). Who you know and how you know them can have a huge influence on the quality of the final negotiated outcome. An important feature which characterizes relationships is the extent to which the relational partners trust each other. The professional and popular literature portrays trust as the social glue which makes our relationships with others possible – and workable. It is also the oil which lubricates the financial system and the magic remedy that can keep partners together, even when everything else seems to be collapsing around them. In short, trust facilitates both effective and productive relationships (79).

One of the curious things about trust is that it is a very easy word to use, but often a very difficult concept to apply in practice. Showing trust and giving trust is not always easy. An important reason for this is that trust is very much 'in the eye of the beholder'. Trust is founded on perceptions and evaluations that are not necessarily based on the available objective information. The subjective element frequently plays an important part in deciding whether or not we trust someone. For example, people find it easier to like other people who are similar to them in terms of appearance, tastes, behaviour, and so on – which you can hardly call a rational strategy. In the professional literature trust is defined as 'an individual's belief in, and willingness to act on the basis of, the words, actions and decisions of another' (80).

Trust is therefore the expectation that the intentions and decisions of others will not damage your own interests. In other words, the presence of trust in a relationship is something positive. Perhaps as a result, trust is seen as a valuable asset (81), but one which can only be built up gradually. However, it can be broken in an instant, if your trust is betrayed. Building up trust is easiest when everything is running smoothly. In these circumstances it is easier to get to know each other better and to promote each other's interests. The need for trust is greatest when things start to go wrong. This leads to uncertainty and means that you want confirmation of the reliability of the other party. This uncertainty can be minimized if people take the opportunity to continue building up trust during the good periods. Unfortunately, this does not always happen. As a result, the basis of trust is often insufficient when the relationship hits a crisis. This means that it becomes necessary to start rebuilding that relationship at a difficult moment – and this is never easy. Consequently, it is necessary for a negotiator to understand what the concept of trust means, which elements contribute to our perception of trust and how to deal with distrust.

GIVING TRUST CREATES TRUST

Trust is given and received within the context of a relationship between different parties and is therefore an essential precondition for negotiations. However, this implies that one of the parties must take the risk that starts the trust-building process. A key question is therefore: who will take the first step to develop a trusting relationship? People often say that 'you can only get trust if you give trust'. However, negotiating practice would suggest that most negotiators ignore this well-intentioned advice. On the contrary, they seem to regard healthy suspicion as a more appropriate opening move. It would be naive to do otherwise – or so they claim. But are they really right? We know from research that trust is very fragile. We also know that the way you view trust also has a major influence on the extent to which you yourself will be regarded as trustworthy. This means that it is difficult to establish trust on the basis of minimal commitment.

It is time for another game scenario (82). Imagine that you have 10 pounds and that you can divide this money between yourself and a second party. Every euro that you give to this other party is multiplied by a factor of three. You decide to give him or her 6 pounds. After the multiplication by three, this means that the other party now has 18 euros in their possession, leaving you with just 4 pounds. The other party is now asked to redivide the 18 euros with you. The rules of the game mean that if he or she divides the money fairly and equally (a 9–9 split), you will end up with more money $(4+9=13$ pounds) than if you had not given any money during the first division (in which case, you would have kept just 10 pounds). For this reason, this game is known as 'the trust game': by giving trust you increase the final rewards for both parties. Sounds great, doesn't it? But does it match reality? Is this what people really do?

As you might expect, different people adapt different strategies when playing this game. In general, the object is to ensure that by giving trust you can also maximize your own rewards. One of the most frequently used strategies is designed to achieve an equal final distribution of wealth. This means that you give 2.5 pounds to the other party. Multiplied by three, this gives him or her 7.5 pounds and you also retain 7.5 of the original 10 pounds. You then both agree that he or she should not give you any money during the second division, so that equality is maintained. This strategy is particularly popular with children. It is simple and takes no account on the initial origin/ownership of the money. This preference for simplicity – as opposed to a strategy which would seek to further increase the maximum amounts available to both parties – is attributable to the fact that there is little frontal activity in the brain of a child. Another strategy is just to keep the 10 pounds and give the other person nothing. This is a very negative option, which makes future collaboration almost impossible. Moreover, you create no added value – and this is the very purpose of negotiation.

To achieve this purpose, it will be necessary to take a risk. The risk called 'giving trust'. One possible strategy to achieve this objective is to give the full 10 pounds to the other party. Using the game's multiplication formula, this means that he or she now has 30 pounds at their disposal – and you have nothing. So what should the other party do in this situation? What does he or she do? Research indicates that on average this is the best strategy for maximizing your own final amount. The statistics show that in this scenario more than 50% of people agree to give you back half of the total sum during the second division (83). In other words, you both end up with 15 pounds, which represents a 50% increase on your starting capital. Not bad! However, the studies also indicate that if you give less than the full amount to the other party during the first division, you will never get the full amount back during the second division. This means that if you do not show that you trust the other party fully – by giving him or her everything you have – he or she will not feel motivated to give you your money back when there is the opportunity to do so. For example, if you only give him or her 5 pounds (thereby keeping 5 pounds for yourself), it is very likely that he or she will give you back less than 5 euros in return. As a result, you will end up with less than your original starting capital.

These studies demonstrate in a simple but effective manner that if you wish to communicate your trust to another party, it is better to do so whole-heartedly. If you do not give him or her your full trust, this is almost the same as giving no trust at all. The behaviour of the participants in the trust game illustrates this point clearly. They assumed that if the first person did not give them the full amount, this was because this person did not really trust them. It implied that they might not return half the money during the second division, but would pocket the full 30 pounds for themselves. In other words, the giving of partial trust encourages people to adopt a far more calculating and competitive approach – with all that this might mean in terms of possible double-dealing and exploitation.

These results are also useful for suggesting the extent to which you should rely on contracts from the very beginning of the negotiating process. What is better? To start your discussions with contracts already on the table or only to produce a formal written agreement when the discussions are nearing their end? It is important to realize that working with contracts – which will usually contain all kinds of clauses designed to protect you – communicates to the other party that you do not really trust them. If you did, why would you need all this protection? Making immediate use of contracts therefore creates a frame in which the negotiations will be viewed exclusively as 'business' (see Chapter 5). Negotiations which are viewed through this 'business' lens will usually be conducted on the basis of calculated thinking. The relational aspects will be much less important and it is not really possible to speak of 'trust'. Nor is it realistic to think that you can get the best of both worlds by working with contracts whilst at the same time adopting a more relational approach. It is either one or the other. With this distinction: the use of a relational approach from the beginning of the negotiations will give you the opportunity to win the confidence and trust of the other party. And if you can achieve this, you will later be able to discuss openly and honestly how the matters on which you agree can best be set down in a contract. In contrast, opening the discussions with a whole series or restrictive rules and regulations simply creates mistrust and consequently makes the negotiations that much more difficult (84).

REPAIRING TRUST

A major threat to negotiations is the possibility that the trust which you have built up – often with such difficulty – can be damaged. This can easily occur. There is a well-known saying which warns us that 'it can take ages to build up trust, but just a single second to destroy it'. If or when this happens, it is important to realize that this damage can take one of two forms. Firstly, there is the negative form: we gave someone our trust and they have shown themselves not to be worthy of it. Secondly, there is the positive form: we expected that someone was not to be trusted, but they have proven us wrong and are now offended that we doubted them. What these two forms have in common is the fact that there is a discrepancy between expectation and result. If this discrepancy becomes too great, then we can speak of a breach of trust. In general, people are more strongly affected by their negative experiences than by their positive ones, and therefore take greater account of their negative experiences in their evaluation of situations (85). For this reason, the damage to existing trust (negative) will weigh more heavily than the existence of doubts about the other party's trustworthiness (positive) and will have a correspondingly greater influence on your future relations. Consequently, it is on negative damage that we will focus in this section.

When trust is damaged, we revert to a situation of distrust. Distrust is characterized by a high degree of uncertainty. You no longer know what the other party is thinking or planning. It is difficult to decide which information is accurate and which is not. In other words, distrust leads to ambiguity with regard to the intentions of your negotiating partner. As already mentioned, people have an aversion for this type of uncertainty. Ironically enough, however, it is precisely this aversion that can help you to rescue the situation. Because people are 'programmed' to avoid or at least reduce uncertainty, they have a strong need to trust others. If you can trust the other person, you no longer need to fear the risk of possible exploitation. You can meet each other across the negotiating table with openness and honesty. It is therefore important that every negotiator should know how trust can best be repaired, once it has been damaged.

An important first principle is that we should always try to interpret a breach of trust in a positive manner. All too often, we look at such matters exclusively in negative terms, which means that we fail to explore the potential still offered by the situation. 'What potential?' I can hear you ask. Namely, the potential to show that, after all, you really are a partner that can be trusted. During crisis situations of this kind, there is always great uncertainty about what you can expect from the other party. In these situations, the actions which people take are always viewed diagnostically, with the purpose of assessing what they are really like. Why do we do this? Imagine that you are in a situation where everything is running smoothly. There is no crisis and everyone is making a positive contribution. In these circumstances, it is very difficult to establish whether or not your partners can be fully trusted. Some of them might be playing games – but how can you find out? At the present time, no one's self-interest is being threatened and so there is no need for competitive behaviour, which might reveal more about their true intentions. Everyone is being cooperative, and this type of 'easy' behaviour makes it difficult to judge people accurately. The reverse is true in crisis situations. This is when the gloves really come off, so that what people say and what people do is a more reliable diagnostic tool for assessing their true personality. A crisis forces you to openly defend your own interests, but if you can do this in a manner which still aims to be essentially cooperative; this will say a great deal about your ultimate trustworthiness.

In other words, a breach of trust can actually create a situation in which it is possible to show the world (and your negotiating partners) the 'real' and reliable you. For this reason, it is vital that you should know how to react when this opportunity arises. The most important thing is to try and show in a sincere and genuine manner that you are prepared to work hard to change the existing situation of distrust; that you are prepared to do this in order to earn (or earn back) the trust of the other parties. In short, you must show that you are willing to 'go the extra mile'; that you are willing to make sacrifices to restore people's confidence in each other. And you must do all this with a smile on your face. Don't moan about it; just do it! This is by far the most effective strategy.

THE VALUE OF AN APOLOGY

During negotiations, it is inevitable that comments and accusations will be made that do little to improve the relations between the negotiating parties. Quite the reverse! Accusations of this kind are often made because promises have not been kept. As a result, the parties may adopt a more defensive attitude, so that the negotiations become less constructive. The easiest reaction to an accusation is a denial. No one likes to take responsibility when things are going wrong, particularly if the finger is being pointed at you. Yet while denial is an understandable response, it is not necessarily the best one. To date, research has only identified a limited number of situations in which a denial can actually have a positive effect. For example, studies suggest that in cases relating to breach of integrity – or when other 'moral' issues are at stake – it is usually better to deny the accusation than to admit it (86). This is because people (need to) see integrity as something stable. If you once show that your integrity is not to be trusted, it will be very difficult to shake off this tarnished image. And so it is better to lie or deny – but do not apologize. Recent surveys have shown that people who are firmly convinced that morality is a stable personal characteristic are most influenced by denials (87). Of course, your denial must be plausible. Other surveys indicate that your initial denial will rebound against you if subsequent evidence of your 'guilt' can easily be found.

But there is another, and perhaps better, approach. If you are looking to win people's trust, you must be prepared to take responsibility for your actions. You must be prepared to admit to the other negotiating partners that you have made a mistake. This admission should also be accompanied by an apology. An apology which is sincerely and correctly given can go a long way towards repairing any damage which may have been caused. The reason for this is that an apology will influence the other person's perception of you in a positive manner. And as we have already mentioned: 'trust – like beauty – is in the eye of the beholder'. It is therefore important that the guilty party should own up to his or her actions and even offer some explanation for them. In this way, he or she can persuade the offended party to forgive him or her.

A whole battery of studies has shown that the offering of an apology can be an effective way to repair damaged relations (88, 89). Notwithstanding this good news, however, a degree of caution is necessary. First of all, we need to remember that apologies are not always given. This means that there must be thresholds which prevent or discourage people from apologizing. Second, it is important to realize that not all apologies are effective at restoring relations in a manner which will allow the negotiations to continue smoothly. It is therefore necessary to know *when* and *why* an apology can achieve the desired results.

With regard to the *when*, research suggests that most people adopt a strategic approach. For example, the majority of guilty parties will only offer an apology if they think that there is a good chance that they will be forgiven (87). If the offended party has a reputation as being someone who finds it difficult to forgive, the apology will usually be withheld. This can have consequences for the way the parties deal with each other during the negotiations. It means that the restoration of trust will be effected in an instrumental manner. On the one hand, the guilty party will only admit to their mistake if they think that it is likely to be to their advantage, that is, that they will be forgiven. On the other hand, it means that the offended party may try to mask their tough negotiating style. If he or she comes across as too hard and too unforgiving, the required apology may never be forthcoming. All he or she will get is denials.

Moreover, it has been shown that the offering of an apology can also negatively affect the self-image of the apologizing party (90). A strongly positive self-image means that people are full of confidence and are generally more successful. People feel good if they can look at themselves in a positive light. As might be expected, such people are highly motivated to maintain this high level of self-esteem. Unfortunately, acceptance of responsibility for a breach of trust is not something of which you can be proud. It makes clear that you have failed, have made a mistake. It is hardly surprising that you are reluctant to apologize for this!

This is where the offended party can help. They need not refrain from asking for an apology, but they should do so in a manner which allows the guilty party to maintain their dignity and self-respect. If, on the contrary, you attempt to take the moral high ground – in short, if you attempt to rub the guilty party's nose in it – you can wait for your apology until the cows come home.

With regard to the question of *why* apologies work, it is necessary to keep a number of different points in mind. To maximize your apology's effectiveness, you need to devote attention to the way in which you apologize, to the content of your apology and to the circumstances in which it is given. Apologies must make clear that the guilty party is sorry for what has happened, and that he or she understands the consequences this has had for the offended party. This means that he or she accepts the need to bear responsibility for these consequences (91). Apologies which express regret but which, nevertheless, try to pass the blame on to someone else are not a good idea. They will usually work against you, because they create the impression that you are not sincere. And sincerity is a basic condition for a successful apology. When do people consider an apology to be sincere? To begin with, when it is offered spontaneously, with a minimum of delay and not in response to social pressure. It is also a great help if the parties concerned do not have a past history of conflict. A first apology to someone also has a much greater effect than a fifth, sixth, or seventh apology. By this stage, your apologies no longer have much credibility!

Which circumstances can help to assure that your apology is well received? A key factor in all aspects of the negotiating process is the showing of proper respect to the other parties, even if your basic values and norms are fundamentally different (see Chapter 2). This is not only necessary to create a constructive atmosphere, but it also helps to rebuild trust once it has been damaged. Research has confirmed that apologies are seen as more sincere and more well-meant if the guilty party has respect for the offended party (92, 89). The effectiveness of an apology is also dependent upon the extent to which the breach of trust involves a failure of competence or a failure of integrity. If it is apparent that trust has been damaged because the guilty party did not have the necessary competencies to meet a particular situation, then an apology is strongly recommended. If the damage has been caused by a lack of integrity on the part of the guilty party, the apology will carry much less weight (see also our reasoning above on the use of denials).

In summary, the offering of an apology has several advantages, providing that your apology can satisfy a number of basic conditions. In particular, it must contain a number of elements that have a positive practical effect of your relations with the other negotiating parties. An effective apology therefore shows:

- That you regret what has happened: 'I am sorry.'
- That you accept your responsibility: 'I have made a mistake.'
- That you are sincere and want to make amends: 'I want to do my best to put things right.'
- That you find it important to be forgiven by the offended party: 'Can you forgive me?'

- That you offer an explanation for your behaviour and do not try to put the blame on someone: 'I did it because...'
- That you will not repeat this behaviour in the future: 'I promise that I won't do it again.'
- That you know how you will behave in similar circumstances in future: 'Next time this happens, I will...'

Notwithstanding the many advantages attached to apologies, it should not be forgotten that an apology is only a first step in the much longer process of rebuilding damaged trust. Very recent research indicates that many offended parties strongly overestimate the effect of an apology on their own reactions (93). In other words, once the apology has been received, people are often less satisfied than they had anticipated. This underlines the fact that an apology must always be accompanied by a genuine change in behaviour. Just saying sorry is not enough! As previously stated, an apology implies promises and commitments. These must be carried out in full in as transparent a manner as possible.

COMPENSATING PEOPLE FOR FINANCIAL LOSS

We now know that the restoration of broken trust is a complex matter, which requires more than a simple admission of guilt. You need to take effective action which 'legitimizes' your apology and makes restitution for any material and financial loss which you may have caused.

In many formal negotiation situations this latter aspect – the financial one – plays a crucial role. For example, in negotiations to form a new government the potential coalition partners are primarily concerned with a combination of symbolic and financial issues. This inclusion of a financial component means that trust in this context needs to be interpreted in a more economic or calculated manner (see Chapter 5 on framing effects). In a more purely financial context, trust is regarded as the oil which is necessary to facilitate financial transactions. Relationships are seen largely as economic transactions. This means that trust can almost literally be expressed in figures. Loss figures mean less confidence; profit figures mean more confidence.

Research into the role of trust in financial negotiations indicates that up to a certain point a breach of confidence can be repaired by the payment of financial compensation (94, 95). An important question in this respect is whether the restoration of trust means that you should simply compensate the value of the financial loss or whether you actually need to pay something extra, almost like a kind of moral damage indemnity. Because the breach of trust also contains a symbolic element – you are losing not only money but also your psychological sense of security – the payment of additional 'moral' compensation is more advisable. This shows that you understand the pain felt by the other party and that you are prepared to do something extra to put things right. However, if the guilty party is the strongest party in the relationship, they may feel inclined to ignore this symbolic aspect altogether. For this reason, they will usually only pay exact compensation – although this can sometimes work against them in the long term (see Chapter 7).

A series of different studies have already demonstrated how and why overcompensation can frequently achieve good results. Overcompensation can certainly be an effective way to restore trust, but only if the motives of the guilty party are not clear to the offended party. For example, if as the guilty party you were attempting something fraudulent, all the overcompensation in the world will not help to restore the lost trust. However, if your motives are less obvious or less unacceptable, there is still a chance to show that you are worthy of being trusted. In this latter case, the payment of financial compensation shows that you meant – and mean – well. In other words, it does not pay to be too transparent about the reasons which led you to damage the trust in the first place. Other research has shown that if a third party – a judge or an arbitrator – forces the guilty party to make financial restitution for the damage caused, the payment of overcompensation is no more effective than the payment of exact compensation. The opposite is true if the overcompensation is offered spontaneously. This communicates sincerity and a sense of genuine regret, which is never possible with compulsory payments.

Finally, it should be noted that the payment of financial compensation is not always the best method to restore trust in economic negotiations (96). If the negotiations relate to the division of expenditure and losses, financial compensation is certainly the most effective way to regain lost confidence. But if the negotiations relate to the division of profits and gains, well-meant apologies are the best way to get things back on track. The loss frame focuses attention strongly on self-interest, which means that a purely financial approach will be seen as a more valuable response than attempting to repair the damaged relationship with an apology. In contrast, the gain frame concentrates more closely on the relational aspects of the situation, so that the payment of cash is regarded as less appropriate than the expression of heartfelt regrets.

This may suggest that the best strategy to restore lost trust is to combine the payment of financial compensation with a sincere apology. Recent research has shown that the effectiveness of this combination depends upon the different parties' perception of the negotiating situation (97). In some circumstances, an apology can be interpreted as a sign of weakness, so that it is wiser to stick to purely financial compensation. In other circumstances, a wad of cash may not satisfy the relational requirements of the offended party and may even be regarded as some kind of bribe. Other studies indicate that purely financial compensation works better if the breach of trust has occurred between two individuals. However, the addition of an apology can enhance the effectiveness of financial compensation if the offended party is an individual but the guilty party consists of more than one person (i.e., is a group).

CHAPTER 7

POWER

As soon as negotiations begin between two or more people, the processes and mechanisms of power come into play. Power means that one party possesses qualities to compel another party to do something that this other party would never do voluntarily. Possessing power therefore allows you to exercise influence, so that you can achieve your objectives more easily. You are better able to form coalitions, obtain information or impose deadlines. It is important to realize, however, that in the longer term the exercising of too much power will have more negative rather than positive effects. Your relations with others can become sour, which might make it difficult to keep the negotiations going in a constructive manner. If you behave like a dictator, you may get your own way this time, but you will create little goodwill and trust for the future. On the contrary, you will acquire a bad reputation. For this reason, it is essential to use your power only if another party persists in defending an unacceptable position – and needs to be 'persuaded' to see reason. As a negotiator, it is therefore necessary to know what kind of power you possess and also what advantages and disadvantages they bring with them.

Power can take various forms. French and Raven make a distinction between five different sources of power which can be important for negotiators: legitimate power, the power to reward, the power to coerce, the power of the expert, and the power of the referent (98).

- *Legitimate power* is the power that a negotiator can exercise as a result of his or her position and status. The higher your position in the hierarchical ladder, the more power you will have over others, viewed in objective terms. It needs to be emphasized that this type of power is only seen by others as being legitimate if its holder also possesses good interpersonal qualities; for example, if he or she treats others in a procedurally correct manner and shows them respect.
- A negotiator possesses the *power to reward* if he or she is in a position to recompense another party for their cooperation. This type of power makes it easier to win the support of others. Thanks to the principle of reciprocity, someone who is rewarded will be more inclined to view your future requests in a more positive light.
- The *power to coerce* is the opposite of the power to reward. This type of power allows you to deny another party access to information or certain services. It also allows you to discipline others if they fail to keep their promises. To understand the influence of this kind of power, it is important to know how 'absolute' your position of power really is. If your power is not absolute, you need to be careful about how you coerce or punish people. Punishment always triggers negative reactions and can lead to a desire for revenge. In the long run this can have disastrous consequences for your position – particularly if it is not generally regarded

as legitimate and stable. Even if your power is absolute, it is still advisable to be fair and selective with your punishment. Otherwise, you will quickly acquire a reputation as a dictator. This can work against you if in subsequent negotiations you need to work with people who have equal power.

■ The *power of the expert* is held by people who possess knowledge and qualities which the other negotiating parties need. This type of power is characteristic of the power base around which most negotiating coalitions are formed. The different parties often agree to work together because they need each other's different and complementary skills. In other words, a combination of different types of expertise is necessary. The party with the greatest level of expertise will, by definition, have the strongest position of power within the resulting coalition. It is important to realize that while this type of power is very useful, it is also highly relative. As the negotiations move forward, new problems requiring new experts will inevitably arise. The power of the expert is not, therefore, a stable power base.

■ The *power of the referent* is held by people who possess certain charismatic qualities in combination with an excellent positive reputation. This type of power means that people will be more willing to listen to you, because they regard you as an ideal leader. In other words, you are a trendsetter who sets an example to be followed by others. This power also gives you the power to impose social punishments on others. If you decide to exclude a particular party, the remaining parties will easily accept this.

POWER AND YOUR UNDERSTANDING
OF THE OTHER PARTY

It has already been mentioned more than once: it is vital for a negotiator to prepare everything thoroughly in advance. Good preparation means that you need to pay attention to even the smallest details. You need to know the weaknesses of the other party, you need to know what the other party wishes to achieve and you need to assess how far these objectives are compatible with your own. If your position of power is relatively strong, you will probably find it easier to gather and process all this information. In other words, power can help to ensure that your preparation is superior to that of the other negotiating parties. Or this, at least, is the theory. In practice, it is often very different. Why? Because there is one particularly irritating characteristic of power: it makes it extremely difficult to put yourself in the other person's shoes. The more power you have, the less easy it becomes to see things from the other party's perspective. And this means that you will be less able to evaluate what he or she is thinking, feeling, and doing (99). Moreover, this is an automatic process which is activated as soon as you acquire more power. As a result, its effects are largely unconscious. It is therefore very important for a negotiator to be aware of this fact – and to do something about it.

Recent research has closely charted the relationship between power and the ability to appreciate the other party's perspective (100). Studies show that negotiators in a powerful position interpret the emotions of others less accurately. The ability to identify and interpret emotions is an important quality in a negotiator, since it allows you to better judge the motives and objectives of the other party (see Chapter 4). The recognition and understanding of the implication of emotions likewise allows you to better anticipate how the other party might act. Research has also shown that powerful negotiators assume that their less powerful negotiating partners do not possess the same information as they do. And it is indeed true that powerful negotiators may find it easier to gain access to scarce information. However, it is also possible that less powerful negotiators might also be able to acquire this same information by forming the right coalitions with the right people. In other words, even powerful negotiators need to think carefully about the information that the other side might possess. Do they know as much as him or her? Do they know more than him or her?

Lack of insight into these processes can mean that powerful parties sometimes show a complete lack of understanding towards their weaker colleagues. This can make the relations between the parties more tense than is necessary. Moreover, research results also indicate that powerful negotiators are more prone to think in terms of stereotypes. Stereotypes can be useful up to a certain point, since they allow you to give structure to an excess of information. However, the use of stereotypes also means that you will be likely to process this information in a very general and superficial way. This can work against you, since one of the key characteristics of good preparations is that they allow you to look at the forthcoming negotiations in a detailed and highly concrete manner (101).

A strong position of power is certainly very useful for opening doors that might otherwise have remained closed. But it is important to recognize that a feeling of power can also lead to inefficient tendencies which may totally upset your carefully planned preparations – almost without you even realizing it!

POWER AND FREEDOM OF MOVEMENT

Negotiation is a dynamic activity in which social influence plays a key role. Social pressure and the strategic behaviour of the other side may mean that you are required to take decisions in a manner which is very different to what you had originally intended. Negotiators often experience frustration if they are forced to deviate from the negotiating pathway that they had plotted for themselves during their preparation. It is can also occur that the close of the negotiations leaves you with a negative feeling: a feeling that you were too limited in the way you were able to steer the discussions in the direction you wanted. These types of problems are more commonly the lot of less powerful negotiating parties.

Conceptual analysis has revealed that the idea of 'power' is associated with a greater feeling of freedom, a sense that fewer obstacles are placed in your way and a belief in your ability to obtain better rewards (102). This mindset has important consequences for negotiators – consequences that can bring them numerous advantages. Power makes negotiators more optimistic and less afraid to take risks (103). They feel less restricted by limitations and are therefore more prepared to actually accept risk. Their thought processes are less conservative and this allows them to think 'out of the box'. This creative approach is exactly what is needed if the aim is to increase the size of the pie on the negotiating table (see Chapters 3 and 5).

In addition, a feeling of power also makes it easier to estimate your own future behaviour. A powerful position means that you will face less obstacles, so that you will be less frequently confronted with aggressive and competitive opponents (104). This is greatly to your benefit: negotiators who are more subject to the influence of their opponent's behaviour are less likely to realize their own objectives in full. As a result, the predictions of this kind of negotiator are less accurate. This leads to a situation where you are compelled to adjust your strategy and your expectations. And if you find yourself in a position where it becomes increasingly difficult to make accurate predictions, this can negatively affect your self-confidence.

Power can therefore offer numerous advantages within a negotiating context. For this reason, it is important that each negotiator should ask himself or herself how their own power position can be improved. There are different ways that you can try to achieve this:

■ Make sure that you have plenty of alternatives. This means that you need to make contacts with potential future partners. Develop the habit of having a potential alternative partner in mind for every party with whom you are currently negotiating.
■ Make sure that you have sufficient objective information about the other party. In practice, this often means that you must tap several sources in order to build up a realistic picture of the person on the other side of the negotiating table. For this reason, it is important to maintain contact with various people who know or work for/with the other party.

- Try to make your own social status and expertise clear to the other party during the negotiating process. This might help you to stand out from the crowd; as a result, you may be viewed in a more positive light than the others. Be careful, however, that your behaviour does not appear to be too explicit: arrogance of this kind can arouse negative feelings instead of positive ones.
- Try to make your behaviour as consistent as possible, irrespective of time, place, and person. This sends out a clear signal to the other negotiators which says that you know why you are there and what you are doing. In this way, you will come across as someone who believes in his or her own abilities. This can only help to make a favourable impression on the other party.
- Try to be the negotiator who stresses the general good. Emphasize the need to create a win–win situation. This cooperative attitude will strengthen your moral status within the negotiations.

While these are all useful tips, it is not always possible to apply them successfully. Many of these strategies involve maintaining contacts in the camp of the other party. This means that you will also need a strong personality to persuade these contacts to move in the direction you want them to go. If you do not possess this quality, you may need to rely on the following:

- Try to improve your BATNA.
- Try to identify the weaknesses of the other party and exploit them when necessary.
- Avoid creating the impression that you are in a weak negotiating position.

- Try to frame decisions in such a way that they always appear to be moral decisions.
- Try to build up a coalition.

POWER CAN MAKE YOU BLIND

We have already made the point: power can bring you numerous advantages in a negotiating context. Nevertheless, it is important to remain aware of the cognitive errors that can be induced by too much power. People have a natural tendency to acquire power and to use it. And it is precisely this tendency that can blind people to the effects of power, in such a way that it can actually undermine the position they are so eager to preserve. Once the differences in relative levels of power become clear, the most powerful party becomes more likely to deal with potential problems in looser, less structured manner. In fact, you might even say that excessive power is inclined to make you lazy. But why is this so? Do you simply overestimate your own strength? Or do you underestimate the strength of others? Research has confirmed that this second assertion is the correct one: if we are too powerful, we consistently undervalue the strength of the other party (105). For this reason, powerful parties are inclined to treat less powerful parties with a lack of respect (see Chapter 6, and the importance of respect for the restoration of trust). The dividing line between assertiveness and arrogance is never far away.

In these circumstances, it is hardly surprising that the reactions of the other party are focused on undermining the position of the strongest party. Consequently, the message for the strongest parties is that they must do what they can to remove any reasons which might provoke other parties to challenge their position of power. For example, even though power gives you the ability to easily influence the benefits which are allocated to others at the end of the negotiating process, it is, nonetheless, advisable to adopt a more understanding approach towards the different interests of the other parties. It is equally advisable to try and maintain good relations with everyone and to stress that you are interested in promoting the common good, notwithstanding your powerful position. This attitude will help to eliminate or minimize the negative feelings of the other parties. In other words, mutual trust will not suffer as a result of the existing distribution of power.

In addition, it is also important to keep questioning your own qualities and abilities. In this respect, it is important to realize that you should try to use your power to bring the interests of the different parties closer together. Power is not simply a question of rights, that is, the right to exercise your power. It is also a question of responsibility, that is, the responsibility to exercise your power wisely. This means, amongst other things, that you should use your power in such a way that it promotes and maintains mutual trust and harmony. If you forget to do this, in the long run you may arouse the hostility of the other parties, so that they try to chip away at your power base.

All these facts lead to a simple general conclusion: once you have acquired a position of power, it is important to maintain it through judicious and appropriate behaviour. Never assume that the mere possession of power is enough by itself. Power is not an end but a means to an end. Consequently, you must continuously question and evaluate your position, bearing in mind the interests of other weaker parties. If you can achieve this delicate balancing act, it will allow you to maximize the benefits of the negotiating process – not just for yourself, but for all concerned.

ACQUIRING OTHER PEOPLE'S POWER: ASKING FOR FAVOURS

The different parties in a negotiation process each possess different levels of power and status. These differences in power are usually built up over a period of time and are established before the negotiations begin. But it is also possible to acquire additional power while the negotiations are actually in progress. This 'new' power can be gained by making good use of the principle of reciprocity. This principle is based on the precept that if you do a favour for another party, this other party will respond in kind. Or as the old adage puts it: 'You scratch my back, and I'll scratch yours.' This is a technique that is particularly popular in the United States, where, for example, it has become a tradition for companies to offer financial support to various different kinds of organizations. This is not philanthropy: the real purpose of these donations is to obtain favours from the organizations in question. In the United States this method of business is known as lobbying and is perfectly acceptable. In many other countries it is known as bribery and is often a criminal offence. Be that as it may, this difference in perception shows how the game of giving support and asking for favours is closely related to the building up of positions of power.

So how exactly does this work? A popular negotiating technique is to ask one of the other parties for a big favour. This favour must be sufficiently exaggerated, so that there is every chance that the other party will refuse. But this is precisely the essence of the game. As soon as the other party says 'no', you need to react decisively. Suggest that you meet again to examine how the matter can be approached differently. This immediately creates an opening for further discussion. When you eventually get together, be ready with an offer of your own that you know will interest the other party. This might be a gift (tickets to U2 or the Cup Final) or a concession that you were already planning to make. Make sure that what you are now putting on the table can be seen as something separate and wholly unrelated to the favour which you originally asked. If the other party accepts this 'bait', it immediately puts them in a position where they feels obliged to do something in return for you. This is the moment to reintroduce your original request. The principle of reciprocity means that there is now a much bigger chance that your wishes will be granted. People are amazingly sensitive to the idea that if they receive something, they must give something in return. Yet perhaps this is hardly surprising. Evolutionary history teaches us that people who do not adhere to the reciprocity principle are eventually excluded from society – with all the negative consequences that this entails.

The advantages of this tactic are clear. By taking the initiative and asking for an exaggerated favour, you ensure that the other party enters into discussions. By provoking the rejection of your request, you give yourself the opportunity to do something relatively minor for the other party, in order to 'make amends'. If the other party accepts this gesture, you can then trap them with the principle of reciprocity. When this happens, the other party becomes more dependent on you than they was before, which effectively increases your power.

To make this tactic work to maximum effect, you need to begin the negotiations with a list of favours you want to ask and corresponding list of gifts/concessions you are willing to give. Remember that reciprocity does not always work as easily as our example suggests. Much depends on the level of the other party's interest in the things you have to offer. The bigger your list and the more flexibly you use it, the greater your chances of success. Remember above all that you need to ensure that your original request is not immediately granted. Were this to happen, you would be unable to create the relationship of dependence that will increase your level of negotiating power.

Closely related to how you want to appear in a negotiation is the use of promises and threats. People sometimes use threats to appear strong, and when they are frustrated. They also make promises when they find that the other party is sceptical about them. What is the impact of these tactics?

PROMISES AND THREATS

During political negotiations, we see negotiators attempt to defuse potential problems or stalemates by making promises. This is done to encourage the opposing party to adopt a more positive approach. If this does not work, it may occasionally be necessary to resort to more serious tactics – such as refusing to honour other promises that you may have previously made. In extreme cases, it may even be necessary to walk away from the negotiating table. Such measures are intended to increase the pressure on the other party, whilst at the same time sending a clear signal that you are not someone to be trifled with. Remember, however, that this influencing strategy can only work up to a certain level. Remember also that neither tactic should be used lightly.

Threats fit in well with the image of a strong negotiator who knows what he or she wants. This type of negotiator will not allow himself or herself to be pushed around. And research does indeed show that the use of threats often works, providing you are in a strong negotiating position (106). In other words, threats are a strong but intimidating way to exercise influence. For this reason, you need to be careful how you use them. If you overplay your hand, they may eventually rebound against you – and this is not your intention. It is important to realize that any threat which you issue as a negotiator must be capable of clear interpretation by the other side. In other words, they must know exactly why you have made the threat. Even more importantly, the threat must be a realistic one. For example, if you threaten to kill your negotiating opponent, nobody will take you seriously (unless, of course, you have shown in the past that you are capable of such action). Consequently, you should always explain clearly what your threat implies. Say what you will do if your threat is ignored, and when you will do it. If you pay little or no attention to the content and form of your threat, you will lose credibility in the sight of others.

It is also necessary to think carefully about the timing of your threats; at which point in the negotiations will you use them. If you are in a position to issue threats, make sure that you do not use this power too soon. It is a much better strategy to gradually turn up the pressure rather than to prematurely reveal your full strength. Humans are by nature creatures who are capable of adapting to changing situations. And it is this capacity to adapt – even in the most challenging of circumstances – that the negotiator needs to exploit. Once again, however, you must be careful how you go about it. If the other party is not used to more aggressive forms of behaviour, he or she will experience your threats as a shock, almost as a slap in the face. In this instance, he or she will probably become more defensive towards you, which will make it harder instead of easier to get your own way. As a result, it is wiser to issue really strong threats only when the end of the negotiations are in sight. Aggressive behaviour increases the level of distrust between the parties, and this is not something you want at the beginning of the negotiating process. Studies have shown that a failure to keep promises or threats at the beginning of a relationship can often lead to a breach of trust that is impossible to repair (59). Finally, you must remember never to issue threats in combination with strongly negative emotions. Instead, you must concentrate (as we mentioned earlier) on making your threats clear and comprehensible – and the required level of transparency is best achieved with calm and controlled communication.

A more constructive way to exercise influence – but one which is no less compelling and persuasive – is the making of promises. This tactic can be employed when you know with certainty that you have something that the other side desperately wants – almost at any price. This works rather like the old story of the carrot and the donkey: you dangle the carrot in front of the donkey's nose and it moves forward to get it – just as you had planned. Of course, it is again crucial to know when you should produce the carrot – and when not. And as with threats, you need to know how your promises can best be communicated. The making of a promise signals that you are keen to work constructively with your negotiating partners; that you are happy to swap gains and losses, rather than just seeking to impose your will from a position of power. This, too, has been confirmed by research: people prefer to see promises made in situations where the balance of strength between the partners is fairly equal and where the emphasis is on cooperation rather than power politics.

Making promises is particularly important during negotiations which involve several parties. This type of negotiation often leads to coalition forming, and these coalitions are usually based on an exchange of promises between the parties concerned. To keep the coalition together, it is necessary that the promises are effectively implemented. It is also important that you do not make the same promise to different parties, if you cannot keep it for all of them: this will undermine your credibility as a negotiator. Being faithful to these principles will create trust and strengthen the collaboration between you and your partners.

Because your willingness to honour your promises is so important in this context, it is essential that you and your partners are very clear with regard to precisely what has been promised. Remember, however, that it is equally important – if not more so – to specify what you have not promised. This requires transparent communication. Tell your partners in which matters you are prepared to support them, but be conscious of the fact that the situation is different if you only promise to support them upon condition that they do something for you in return. This requires even more precise communication. You might think that the *quid pro quo* is inherent in what you have agreed, but in the heat of negotiation the key nuances are not always expressed in unambiguous terms. This often leads to misunderstanding, which can be interpreted as a failure to keep your word. The results are not difficult to imagine: the negotiations fail to run as smoothly as expected, with everyone blaming everyone else and putting forward their own interpretation as the only 'correct' one. In these circumstances, a promise can actually lead to an escalation – rather than a relaxation – of tension.

In order to avoid this damaging ambiguity, make sure that you put clear and precise questions when one of your partners makes you a promise. These questions will allow you to make the promise more concrete. Specific querying with regard to any conditions attached to the promise will help you to further limit the room for potential misunderstanding. If a promise is too general, it often turns out to have much less content at a concrete level than you had expected. Being explicit with your own promises and demanding the same from your partners will help you to prevent irritation and disappointment.

Is it possible to combine the use of threats and promises? It certainly seems logical to assume that you will be able to exercise greater influence if you can apply both tactics simultaneously. This is in keeping with the famous advice once offered by the great American president Franklin D. Roosevelt: 'Talk softly, but carry a big stick.' This effectively means that you can tell your negotiating partners that you are willing to negotiate, but not at all costs. If their promises turn out to be false, you must be prepared to strike back – and they will have no reason to be surprised when you do. Research has confirmed that this type of dual approach – the combination of threats and promises – produces the best results when the negotiating parties are dependent on each other. The effect is greatest when the initial attitude of both sides is focused on cooperation and equality (107).

Where does this all lead us? The single most important conclusion is that in matters of this kind interpersonal relations are crucial. The different parties must show each other the necessary respect. This will create an atmosphere in which open and transparent communication is possible. At the same time, it is equally important that you should make clear to all concerned where your strength lies – and that you will not be afraid to use this strength, if required.

CHAPTER 8

FAIRNESS

There are many situations where negotiators talk about fairness. Negotiators may claim that what they are asking for is fair or that the other party is being unfair. The claims may relate to outcomes or to process and are often the basis for failure to reach mutually beneficial outcomes. Perceptions of fairness, or more accurately unfairness, are often accompanied by negative emotions. These negative emotions override individuals' impulses to look for a good bargain leading them to 'irrationally' reject a seemingly good outcome. A good example of where fairness issues override the desire for self-gain is the ultimatum game that we discussed in the first chapter. In this game, people reject small offers (that are clearly of some value) and take nothing for themselves in order to ensure fairness.

There are many examples of people turning down perfectly good outcomes because they violate their sense of fairness. Unions go on strike to reject unfair wage deals even though the concessions they extract by going on strike do not equal the wages lost on account of the strike (108). Similarly, countries are recalcitrant in international negotiations and give up good deals to enforce the principle of fairness (109). Most of us have some experience of individuals giving up a good outcome in a negotiation because they felt that it violated some sense of fairness. Most of us can therefore agree that fairness is a desirable ideal in negotiations.

However, the issue of fairness in negotiations is not straightforward. Specifically, it is not as easy as saying that negotiations are smooth and agreements sustainable if people behave fairly. Why? There are three parts to the answer to this question. First, there is no one objective and universal criterion to determine fairness in most negotiations. So, people have different interpretations of what is fair in a particular interaction. Second, people choose the criterion that gives them the best possible outcome as the one that determines fairness (a strange notion, and one that we will explore in greater detail in a minute). Thus, people recruit fairness arguments to support their position and weaken others' claims on resources. And, third, people become attached to the criterion that they have come up with. So, they fail to see the legitimacy of the other side's fairness claims. These three features lead to situations where all parties to a negotiation may believe that they are acting fairly; however, the net result is intractable conflict rather than a smooth resolution (110).

Let's begin the discussion with an example. One of the authors of this book was once called in to resolve a dispute between brothers who came from a landowning family. The three brothers had inherited farmland from their father. The land was in their ancestral village where one of the three brothers resided. The other two had jobs in cities (one of them in another country) and had asked their locally resident brother to take care of their property. He did. But over the course of many years, he kept money that was due to his brothers for himself. When the brothers discovered the scale of misappropriation, they took control of their land and attempted to get their 'lost' money back. They were naturally aggrieved that their own brother had cheated them and were demanding restitution. The locally resident brother challenged their claim for back payment. The brothers came to the author as a final resort become going to the courts. When asked to explain the problem, each side used the language of fairness. The locally resident brother claimed that he had taken the money because he *needed* it more than the other two. He claimed that the other two had fairly good incomes from their jobs, and it was therefore fair for him to have kept a large share of the income from their land. The city dwellers claimed that the income from the land needed to be distributed in proportion to their holdings and that the income from their jobs was not relevant to the distribution. They further asked whether it was fair that they should subsidize their brother for his inability to get a good job and income – clearly their preferred criterion of distribution was equality. Each side rigidly adhered to their claim while making it clear that they thought that they were fair and the other side was not.

The example neatly illustrates the three points we would like to make in this chapter. The presence of multiple criteria to determine fairness allows each brother to claim that they were being fair. Each side also picked the criterion that gave them the good outcome – the brother claiming that distribution should be based on need clearly benefits if need is used to distribute resources while the brothers claiming that equality was the legitimate criterion benefit if equality is used as the criterion. And once they had arrived at a determination that they were being fair, they refused to see the other person's point of view.

MULTIPLE LEGITIMATE CRITERIA TO DETERMINE FAIRNESS IN NEGOTIATIONS

Morton Deutsch was one of the most influential psychologists of the twentieth century. Among his many insights was the recognition that there is more than one criterion that one can use to judge that an outcome is fair in any given situation (111). He identified three criteria that he thought were the most widespread – equity or proportionality, equality, and need. Each of these criterion, he said, could be justified based on the goals of the social system in which they were enacted.

Equity is based on the idea of just deserts – each person is rewarded according to their effort or contribution (112). Specifically, if a person contributes more to a joint project, they deserve to get more of the reward. This criterion is the basis of reward allocation in capitalist societies and can be the basis on which we can reach agreement in a negotiation. Imagine a situation in which you and your colleague have created a joint outcome that is being rewarded. You are in a negotiation attempting to distribute the reward and may want to reach an agreement where the person who has made the greater contribution gets the greater reward. Sounds easy, right? Well, here comes the rub. While contribution typically comes in the form of effort (or time), ability or talent might also play a role.

Take, for example, an entrepreneurial team that is in dispute about how to share the potential proceeds from exiting a business. The creative force behind the venture may claim that he or she deserves a larger share despite working only as hard as the others because there would be no business without his or her talent. Other team members may disagree and point out that people should get rewarded according to the time they put into the venture. So, what should we agree is the right input? Is it talent or is it hard work? People who are talented will pick talent and people who have put in the effort will pick effort. But we are running ahead of ourselves here. This is an example of egocentric biases, which we will discuss in detail in the Section 'Egocentric interpretations of fairness in negotiations'.

The second widely accepted criterion is equality. It is simply an even distribution of benefits and burdens without regard to the effort that people put into the joint production. Negotiations will be straightforward if parties can agree to share the benefits or rewards equally (113–115). Academic research suggests that people are more likely to agree to the equality rule when negotiating over the distribution of burdens (e.g., budget cuts spread across departments) or the allocation of non-monetary benefits (e.g., leave or sick benefits in employment relationships). However, this is not a rule that people agree on for every distribution as there would be no incentive to put in more effort if people are given rewards equally without regard to the effort. Hence, the limited applicability of the rule.

The third criterion is need. This particular rule is viewed with suspicion in capitalist societies where rationality demands that we allocate outcomes to increase efficiency. However, here too, most people would agree, and research shows that they agree, that kidneys (or other organs) should be given to the most needy rather than to the most worthy.

Research shows that societies vary on the degree to which they subscribe to one criterion rather than the other (7). For example, people from Western countries (notably the United States) subscribe more to the equity criterion while those from Asian countries (notably China) put more emphasis on equality or need. However, regardless of society, most people appear to be egocentric in their adherence to a particular rule.

EGOCENTRIC INTERPRETATIONS OF FAIRNESS IN NEGOTIATIONS

As noted above, people may dispute what constitutes appropriate input into a joint venture. People who put in more effort may claim that they deserve a greater share of a joint outcome while those who have more talent may claim that they have added more value and therefore deserve a lion's share of the outcome. This is what we mean by egocentrism.

Even if we agree about what is the appropriate input, we have the problem of picking the distribution criteria. Research shows that people will generally prefer a distribution rule that gives them the better outcome. People generally think that the equality criterion is the just one for the allocation of outcomes if they are low contributors to joint production and the equity norm is the fair one if they are the high contributors. Note the similarity of the example of the three brothers to this research – the brothers whose need was the highest thought that the need criterion was the fair one. Also note that these preferences are not strategic in that people do not pick a criterion as an appropriate norm merely because it gives them an advantage; they appear to believe that it is fair.

How do we know that? Academics have conducted several studies (both in the laboratory and in the field) where they show that people demonstrate egocentric perceptions of fairness in negotiation situations (116). Specifically, people on opposite sides of the negotiation pick different outcomes (more often the outcome that gives them an advantage) as fair. And more importantly, the degree of egocentrism predicts the likelihood that the negotiators will fail to reach an agreement. If people were being strategic in their arguments, they would not jeopardize potential good outcomes and continue to stick to their arguments that they are fair and the other side is not. But if they truly believe they are fair, they would be willing to lose a potentially good outcome for the sake of the principle.

BELIEF THAT ONE IS FAIR LEADS TO INFLEXIBILITY IN NEGOTIATIONS

We all have experience of righteous people. Once they believe that they are morally right, they are unwilling to make a compromise. Negotiations founder when the principals to the negotiation believe that fairness is on their side. Take the often vexing negotiations for a treaty on global climate change. Despite near unanimity on the need to cut global emissions, there is no agreement about how this will be achieved. Issues of fairness dominate the discussion with the emerging economies claiming that it is not fair that they are asked to cut emissions even though they have not reached the same levels of per capita emissions as the richer countries. The rich countries, on the other hand, think that it is not fair that the developing world keeps increasing their emissions while they cut down. Compromises are difficult because each party believes that they are right.

If you combine this with the idea that people are often egocentric in their fairness beliefs, then you see the recipe for intractable conflict. Thus, fairness, while important, is often a hindrance to reach an agreement if people pay excessive attention to it.

WHAT WOULD WE RECOMMEND?

- Do not get bogged down in discussions about fairness.
- If the other side makes these arguments:
  - Take their perspective and understand that there is more than one criterion by which we can evaluate fairness;
  - Educate them about the possibility that there is more than one criterion of fairness.

CHAPTER 9

THE 'MOVING FORWARD TO AGREEMENTS' SURVEY*

We began this book by claiming that even though negotiators are not fully rational, they are predictable. People react to situational constraints in systematic ways, and social psychologists have provided us with the necessary tools to predict these ways. We hope that we have persuaded you about this. While we have covered the psychology of negotiations by summarizing extant research on topics such as power, trust, fairness, and emotions and extended them to negotiation interactions, we have left an important part for the end. This is the part about how your behavioural tendencies interact with the negotiation situation to give you the negotiation outcomes that you have been receiving.

An understanding of your behavioural patterns and the way you use it can make the difference between a good final result and a poor one. For this reason, it is advisable to force yourself to continue with your efforts to evaluate the behaviour of others, to understand more fully why the other people act the way they do. Once you have acquired this deeper

---

*© DAVID DE CREMER

144

insight, you will find it easier to make further progress towards your goal: becoming a thoroughly competent negotiator.

In this final chapter you will be introduced to the 'Moving Forward to Agreements' (AMF) Survey. The purpose of this survey is to paint a brief picture of the most important principles which can help your negotiations to run more smoothly at a psychological level. A distinction is made between three different levels. The first level is concerned with the *mindset* of the negotiator. As we have repeatedly mentioned, human beings have certain habits and tendencies which can lead to cognitive errors and less than optimal decisions. It is therefore necessary to regularly check our own psychological mindset. The second level focuses on the actual *process* of the negotiations. Negotiators often forget to form a picture in their own mind of the way they want the negotiations to be structured and how they will relate to the other negotiating parties. In other words, how they will make practical arrangements and use agreed procedures. The third and final level relates to the *end result* of the negotiations. How do you evaluate whether or not these results are satisfactory?

Each level describes a number of principles which can be of benefit to you as a negotiator. You should give a score from 1 to 7 for each of the assertions, depending on the extent to which this assertion appropriately describes your behaviour during the negotiation process.

1 = *totally inapplicable to me*
2 = *not applicable to me*
3 = *not really applicable to me*
4 = *neutral*

5 = *slightly applicable to me*
6 = *applicable to me*
7 = *fully applicable to me*

The lowest score (1) means that your behaviour does not correspond with the principle suggested by the assertion. The highest score (7) means that you fully apply the principle suggested by the assertion. These scores will allow you to identify not only your strong points but also the points on which you need to work further, in order to bring your qualities as a negotiator to a higher psychological level.

LEVEL 1: MINDSET

During negotiations I am someone who...

A. *can always fall back on a clear strategy, which reflects the objective and the final result I want to achieve.*

1	2	3	4	5	6	7

Background: By nature, people are keen to keep things moving forward. For many of us, standing still or marking time is almost a crime! Because of this pressure, many negotiators fail to prepare thoroughly enough. They take too little account of the different ways in which the negotiations can develop. The simulation of different scenarios is often shamefully neglected. Moreover, many negotiators display increasing uncertainty about their own objectives and give a less stable and less convincing impression if the negotiations do not go the way they had anticipated.

B. *does not forget to look at issues from the perspective of the other party.*

1	2	3	4	5	6	7

Background: People focus for 95% of the time on their own perceptions and feelings. This inward-looking focus means that they often fail to encourage the other party to move in their direction. An important aspect of negotiation is the ability to use the perspective of the other party as a basis for evaluating their view of the negotiations.

C. *avoids being influenced by the personality of the other party and tries to stick to rational facts as much as possible.*

1	2	3	4	5	6	7

Background: People have a tendency to attribute the behaviour of the other party to his or her personality. Consequently, the effect of the other party's personality on the negotiations is often overestimated. As a result much objective, relevant and available information is ignored and remains unused during the negotiation process.

D. *is always conscious of the consequences that every small decision can have.*

1	2	3	4	5	6	7

Background: As pressure increases, people are more inclined to behave as if every decision is taken in isolation. This is obviously not the case. The consequences of each decision determine which direction you will take within the framework of the negotiations and which further decisions will need to be made. By underestimating the consequences of decisions negotiators can sometimes cause the situation to escalate, ultimately leading to stalemate. By the time they realize what is happening, it is already too late to do anything about it.

E. *realizes that what is good for me is not necessarily bad for the other party and vice versa. I also communicate this constructive attitude during the negotiations.*

1	2	3	4	5	6	7

Background: Often the parties will quickly come to the conclusion that the offers currently on the table represent the maximum available 'cake' to be divided. This situation can lead to a defensive attitude and encourages competition, without checking to see whether the size of the cake can be increased. Each gain the parties are able to secure is seen as a symbolic victory. It goes without saying that this attitude does not allow the potential inherent in every negotiation to come to full fruition – so that it cannot be used to your advantage.

F. *tries to avoid opting for the easiest solution. I assume that the chance of a 'sweet deal' will not come along every day.*

1	2	3	4	5	6	7

Background: Negotiators who are not well prepared will have a tendency to avoid stress and conflict. Consequently, their highest priority is often to try and feel comfortable within the negotiations. This means, however, that they frequently achieve a less optimal end result.

LEVEL 2: PROCESS

During negotiations, I am someone who ...

A. *always shows respect for the other party, even though we do not share the same values and convictions.*

1	2	3	4	5	6	7

Background: In the commercial world you often hear the expression: 'It's nothing personal, it's just business.' This same reasoning is often used by negotiators. Negotiations are often necessary because people do not share the same values and convictions. If they did, there would be no need to negotiate! However, you must always make every effort to ensure that these differences of opinion and principle are not used to emphasize personal differences. For this reason, it is advisable to 'break the ice' by first talking to the other party about matters such as health, family life or hobbies. This allows you to communicate your respect and interest for the other party through topics that are not directly related to the negotiations.

B. *is prepared to adjust my attitude towards agreed procedures, if the circumstances make it necessary. 'My way or the highway' is very definitely not my motto.*

1	2	3	4	5	6	7

Background: One of the attitudes which can most irritate the other party is a rigid adherence to your own principles or an unwillingness to deviate from previously made agreements. This kind of stubbornness indicates a lack of flexibility and a tendency towards defensive thinking. This is not calculated to win you the sympathy and goodwill of your negotiating partners. Besides, the adjustment of agreements and procedures can sometimes be a useful way to explore other – and perhaps more successful – methods of negotiation.

C. *is more concerned to show trust than to seek absolute control over events.*

1	2	3	4	5	6	7

Background: Creating and keeping trust is one of the most difficult challenges in relationships. Negotiators who try to encapsulate everything in contracts and watertight agreements right from the very start of the negotiations are doomed to failure. This type of behaviour indicates a strong compulsion to control events and will encourage the other party to see you as someone who is not prepared to give trust. Research has shown that precisely the opposite approach is necessary: if you want to receive trust, you must first be willing to trust the other party completely. For this reason, it is not advisable (or realistic) to immediately thrust a contract under the nose of your negotiating partner, whilst at the same time expecting them to give you their trust. These are two contradictory signals, which will do you more harm than good.

D. *tries to ensure that everyone can express their opinion, no matter who they are.*

1	2	3	4	5	6	7

Background: People have a strong desire to express themselves. They need a voice. It will therefore bring you many advantages as a negotiator if you make it possible for others to air their views. This will encourage these others to regard the negotiations as procedurally fair and correct, which in the long run can only increase the level of cohesion between the different parties. Moreover, your willingness to let others have their say will lead to you being seen as a trustworthy and legitimate negotiating partner.

LEVEL 3: END RESULT

During negotiations I am someone who . . .

A. *does not evaluate the end result in a rigid manner. I understand that negotiation is a matter of compromise, which means that the result I achieve will seldom be completely satisfactory.*

1	2	3	4	5	6	7

Background: In the heat of negotiating battle, people often forget that in most cases the end result will be the product of compromise. Negotiation is a game of give and take, so that your personal wishes are not all likely to be granted. Besides, there are several different ways to reach a satisfactory end result. The fact that this does not always happen in the manner that you had envisaged does not mean that the result is necessarily bad.

B. *realize that the end result is best compared with what the outcome would have been if you had not negotiated.*

1	2	3	4	5	6	7

Background: People do not always evaluate the end result in relation to their original starting position, even though this is the only objective and rational comparison to make. If you start with nothing and end with something more, this is clearly progress. Regrettably, people all too often compare their own end result with the end result of other parties or with other negotiation situations that might have given them more. This attitude frequently leads to feelings of disappointment, which can negatively colour their approach towards future negotiations.

C. *does not use my own objectives as the only reference point for the evaluation of the end result.*

1	2	3	4	5	6	7

Background: It is important to round off the negotiations on a positive note. Evaluating the end result exclusively on the basis of your own wishes and preferences will not have this effect. As already mentioned, it is unrealistic to expect to realize all your objectives during the negotiations. If this were possible, it means that your power is already absolute and that negotiations are therefore unnecessary. It is therefore important to realize that the best way to look at the end result is from the perspective of all the parties concerned – including your own. If the general good has been served, the end result can be regarded as successful.

D. *does not make the value of my own end result dependent upon the end result achieved by the other party. If my end result realizes a significant number of the objectives I set for myself, then I am satisfieds.*

1	2	3	4	5	6	7

Background: As social creatures, humans are always inclined to compare themselves with others. Social comparisons not only help us to deal with uncertainties but also allow us to give value to the things we receive and/or achieve. If we compare our own end result too closely with the end result of another party, this can lead to a situation where an objectively good offer is subjectively devalued, which may lead to missed opportunities.

For this reason, it is worth repeating that the only comparison you should make is the comparison between what you had at the start of the negotiations and what you now have upon their conclusion.

REFERENCES

1. Debels, T. (2009). *De ondergang van Fortis* (The extinction of Fortis). Amsterdam: Atlas-Contact.
2. Güth, W., Schmittberger, R., & Schwarze, B. (1982). An experimental analysis of ultimatum games. *Journal of Economic Behavior and Organization, 3,* 367–388.
3. Thompson, L. (2005). *The mind and heart of the negotiator,* 3rd edition. Upper Saddle River, NJ: Pearson Prentice Hall.
4. Raiffa, H. (1982). *The art and science of negotiation.* Cambridge, MA: Harvard University Press/Belknap.
5. Malhotra, D., & Bazerman, M.H. (2007). Investigative negotiation. *Harvard Business Review, 85*(9), September 2007.
6. Shell, R.G. (1999). *Bargaining for advantage: Negotiation strategies for reasonable people.* New York: Viking.
7. Thompson, L., & Loewenstein, G. (1992). Egocentric interpretations of fairness and interpersonal conflicts. *Organizational Behavior and Human Decision Processes, 51,* 176–197.
8. Galinsky, A.D., & Mussweiler, T. (2001). First offers as anchors: The role of perspective-taking and negotiator focus. *Journal of Personality and Social Psychology, 81,* 657–669.
9. Bazerman, M.H., & Carroll, J.S. (1987). Negotiator cognition. In B. Staw & L.L. Cummings (Eds), *Research in organizational behavior* (Vol. 9, pp. 247–288). Greenwich, CT: JAI Press.

10. Samuelson, W.F., & Bazerman, M.H. (1985). The winner's curse in bilateral negotiations. In V. Smith (Ed.), *Research in experimental economics* (Vol. 3, pp. 38–105). Greenwich, CT: JAI Press.
11. Radzevick, J.R., & Moore, D.A. (2008). Myopic biases in competitions. *Organizational Behavior and Human Decision Processes, 107*, 206–218.
12. Ross, L., & Stillinger, C. (1991). Barriers to conflict resolution. *Negotiation Journal, 7*, 389–404.
13. Ross, L. (1977). The intuitive psychologist and his shortcomings: Distortions in the attribution process. In L. Berkowitz (Ed.), *Advances in experimental social psychology* (Vol. 10, pp. 173–220). New York: Academic Press.
14. Diekman, K.A., & Galinsky, A.D. (2006). Overconfident, underprepared: Why you may not be ready to negotiate. *Negotiation, 9*(October), 6–9.
15. Bazerman, M.H., Curhan, J.R., Moore, D.A., & Valley, K.L. (2000). Negotiation. *Annual Review of Psychology, 51*, 279–314.
16. Thompson, L.L. (2008). *The truth about negotiations.* London: Pearson Prentice Hall.
17. Olekalns, M., & Smith, P.L. (2008). Mutually dependent: Power, trust, affect and the use of deception in negotiations. *Journal of Business Ethics, 85*, 347–365.
18. Tenbrunsel, A.E., Wade-Benzoni, K.A., Moag, J., & Bazerman, M.H. (1999). The negotiation matching process: Relationships and partner selection. *Organizational Behavior and Human Decision Processes, 80*, 252–284.
19. Zajonc, R.B. (1968). Attitudinal effects of mere exposure. *Journal of Personality and Social Psychology, 9*, 1–27.
20. Tyler, T.R., & Lind, E.A. (1992). A relational model of authority in groups. In M. Zanna (Ed.), *Advances in experimental social psychology* (Vol. 25, pp. 115–191). New York: Academic Press.

21. Whitener, E.M., Brodt, S.E., Korsgaard, A., & Werner, J.M. (1998). Managers as initiators of trust: An exchange relationship framework for understanding managerial trustworthy behavior. *Academy of Management Review, 23*, 513–530.

22. Vroom, V.H. (1964). *Work and motivation.* New York: Wiley and Sons.

23. De Cremer, D., & Van Knippenberg, D. (2004). Charismatic leadership, collective identification and leadership effectiveness: The interactive effects of leader self-sacrifice and self-confidence. *Organizational Behavior and Human Decision Processes, 95*, 140–155.

24. Locke, E.A., Shaw, K.N., Saari, L.M., & Latham, G.P. (1981). Goal setting and task performance: 1969–1980. *Psychological Bulletin, 90*, 125–152.

25. Coates, J. (1998). *Language and gender: A reader.* Oxford: Blackwell.

26. Vonk, R. (2002). Self-serving interpretations of flattery: Why ingratiation works. *Journal of Personality and Social Psychology, 82*, 515–526.

27. Knapp, M.L., Hopper, R., & Bell, R.A. (1984). Compliments: A descriptive taxonomy. *Journal of Communication, 34*, 12–31.

28. Cialdini, R.B. (2000). *Persuasion: Influence and practice,* 4th edition. New York: Allyn & Bacon.

29. Tversky, A., & Kahneman, D. (1974). Judgment under uncertainty: Heuristics and biases. *Science, 185*(4157), 1124–1131.

30. Carroll, J.S. (1978). The effect of imagining an event on expectations for the event: An interpretation in terms of the availability heuristic. *Journal of Experimental Social Psychology, 14*, 88–96.

31. Neale, M.A. (1984). The effects of negotiation and arbitration cost salience on bargainer behavior: The role of the arbitrator and constituency on negotiator judgment. *Organizational Behavior and Human Decision Processes, 34*, 97–111.

32. Reyes, R.M., Thompson, W.C., & Bower, G.H. (1980). Judgmental biases resulting from differing availabilities of arguments. *Journal of Personality and Social Psychology, 39*(1), July, 2–12.

33. Fischhoff, B., Slovic, P., & Lichtenstein, S. (1978). Fault trees: Sensitivity of assessed failure probabilities to problem representation. *Journal of Experimental Psychology: Human Perception and Performance, 4,* 330–344.

34. Samuelson, W.R., & Zeckhauser, R.J. (1988). Status quo bias in decision making. *Journal of Risk and Uncertainty, 1,* 7–59.

35. Kahneman, D., Knetsch, J.L., & Thaler, R.H. (1991). Anomalies: The endowment effect, loss aversion, and status quo bias. *Journal of Economic Perspectives, 5,* 193–206.

36. De Dreu, C.K.W., & Van Knippenberg, D. (2005). The possessive self as a barrier to constructive conflict management: Effects of mere ownership, process accountability, and self-concept clarity on competitive cognitions and behavior. *Journal of Personality and Social Psychology, 89,* 345–357.

37. Sedikides, C., & Strube, M.J. (1997). Self-evaluation: To thine own self be good, to thine own self be sure, to thine own self be true, and to thine own self be better. In M.P. Zanna (Ed.), *Advances in experimental social psychology* (Vol. 29, pp. 209–269). New York: Academic Press.

38. Kramer, R.M., Newton, E., & Pommerenke, P.L. (1993). Self-enhancement biases and negotiator judgment: Effects of self-esteem and mood. *Organizational Behavior and Human Decision Processes, 56,* 110–133.

39. Bazerman, M.H., & Neale, M.A. (1983). Heuristics in negotiation: Limitations to effective dispute resolution. In M.H. Bazerman & R.J. Lewicki (Eds), *Negotiating in organizations* (pp. 51–67). Beverly Hills, CA: Sage Publications.

40. Neale, M.A., & Bazerman, M.H. (1985). The effects of framing and negotiator overconfidence on bargaining behaviors and outcomes. *Academy of Management Journal*, *28*, 34–49.

41. Kramer, R.M. (1994). Self-enhancing cognitions and organized conflict. Unpublished manuscript.

42. Shafir, E., & Tversky, A. (1992). Thinking through uncertainty: Nonconsequential reasoning and choice. *Cognitive Psychology*, *24*, 449–474.

43. Morris, M.W., Sim, D.L., & Girotto, V. (1998). Distinguishing sources of cooperation in the one-round prisoner's dilemma: Evidence for cooperative decisions based on the illusion of control. *Journal of Experimental Social Psychology*, *34*, 494–512.

44. Messick, D.M., & Sentis, K.P. (1983). Fairness, preference, and fairness biases. In D.M. Messick & K.S. Cook (Eds), *Equity theory: Psychological and sociological perspectives* (pp. 61–64). New York: Praeger.

45. Dees, J.G., & Cramton, P.C. (1991). Shrewd bargaining on the moral frontier: Toward a theory of morality in practice. *Business Ethics Quarterly*, *1*, 135–167.

46. Dees, J.G., & Cramton, P.C. (1995). Deception and mutual trust: A reply to Strudler. *Business Ethics Quarterly*, *5*, 823–832.

47. Trope, Y., & Liberman, N. (2010). Construal-level theory of psychological distance. *Psychological Review*, *117*, 440–463.

48. Staw, B.M. (1976). Knee-deep in the big muddy: A study of escalating commitment to a chosen course of action. *Organizational Behavior and Human Performance*, *16*, 27–44.

49. Arkes, H.R., & Ayton, P. (1999). The sunk cost and Concorde effects: Are humans less rational than lower animals? *Psychological Bulletin*, *125*, 591–600.

50. Northcraft, G., & Neale, M. (1987). Amateurs, experts, and real estate: An anchoring-and-adjustment perspective on property pricing decisions,

Organizational Behavior and Human Decision Processes,
39, 84–97.

51. Bazerman, M.H., Baron, J., & Shonk, K. (2001). *You can't enlarge the pie: Six barriers to effective government.* New York: Basic Books.

52. Adam, H., Shirako, A., & Maddux, W.W. (2010). Cultural variance in the interpersonal effects of anger in negotiations. *Psychological Science, 21,* 882–889.

53. Loewenstein, G. (1996). Out of control: Visceral influences on behavior. *Organizational Behavior and Human Decision Processes, 65,* 272–292.

54. Allred, K.G., Mallozzi, J.S., Matsui, F., & Raia, C.P. (1997). The influence of anger and compassion on negotiation performance. *Organizational Behavior and Human Decision Processes, 70,* 175–187.

55. Pillutla, M.M., & Murnighan, J. (1996). Unfairness, anger, and spite: Emotional rejections of ultimatum offers. *Organizational Behavior and Human Decision Processes, 68,* 208–224.

56. Van Kleef, G.A., De Dreu, C.K.W., & Manstead, A.S.R. (2004). The interpersonal effects of anger and happiness in negotiations. *Journal of Personality and Social Psychology, 86,* 57–76.

57. Karasawa, K. (2001). Anger vs. guilt inference of responsibility and interpersonal reactions. *Psychological Reports, 89,* 731–739.

58. Van Kleef, G.A., De Dreu, C.K.W., & Manstead, A.S.R. (2004). The interpersonal effects of emotions in negotiations: A motivated information processing approach. *Journal of Personality and Social Psychology, 87,* 510–528.

59. Van Dijk, E., Van Kleef, G.A., Steinel, W., & Van Beest, I. (2008). A social functional approach to emotions in bargaining: When communicating anger pays and when it backfires. *Journal of Personality and Social Psychology, 94,* 600–614.

60. Wubben, M., De Cremer, D., & Van Dijk, E. (2009). How emotion communication guides reciprocity: Establishing cooperation through disappointment and anger. *Journal of Personality and Social Psychology, 45*, 987–990.

61. Adler, R., Rosen, B., & Silverstein, E. (1998). Emotions in negotiation: How to manage fear and anger. *Negotiation Journal, 14*, 161–179.

62. Dunn, J., & Schweitzer, M. (2005). Feeling and believing: The influence of emotion on trust. *Journal of Personality and Social Psychology, 88*, 736–748.

63. Goleman, D. (1998). *Working with emotional intelligence.* New York: Bantam Books.

64. Mayer, J.D., Salovey, P., & Caruso, D.R. (2008). Emotional intelligence: New ability or eclectic traits. *American Psychologist, 63*(6), 503–517.

65. Stanovich, K.E., & West, R.F. (2000). Individual differences in reasoning: Implications for the rationality debate? *Behavioral and Brain Sciences, 23*, 645–665.

66. Bazerman, M., & Malhotra, D. (2006). It's not intuitive: Strategies for negotiating more rationally. *Negotiation, 9*(May), 1–2.

67. Dijksterhuis, A., & Nordgren, L.F. (2006). A theory of unconscious thought. *Perspectives on Psychological Science, 1*, 95–109.

68. Pillutla, M., & Chen, X.P. (1999). Social norms and cooperation in social dilemmas. *Organizational Behavior and Human Decision Processes, 78*(2), 81–103.

69. Ross, L., & Samuels, S.M. (1993). *The predictive power of personal reputation versus labels and construal in the prisoner's dilemma game.* Unpublished manuscript. Palo Alto, CA: Stanford University.

70. Kahneman, D., & Tversky, A. (1979). Prospect theory: An analysis of decision under risk. *Econometrica, 47*, 263–291.

71. Bazerman, M.H., Magliozzi, T., & Neale, M.A. (1985). The acquisition of an integrative response in a

competitive market. *Organizational Behavior and Human Decision Processes, 35,* 294–313.

72. Eyal, T., Liberman, L., & Trope, Y. (2008). Judging near and distant virtue and vice. *Journal of Experimental Social Psychology, 44,* 1204–1209.

73. Fujita, K., Trope, Y., Liberman, N., & Levin-Sagi, M. (2006). Construal levels and self-control. *Journal of Personality and Social Psychology, 90,* 351–367.

74. Henderson, M., Trope, Y., & Carnevale, P.J. (2006). Negotiation from a near and distant time perspective. *Journal of Personality and Social Psychology, 91,* 712–729.

75. Henderson, M.D. (2010). Mere physical distance and integrative agreements: When more space improves negotiation outcomes. *Journal of Experimental Social Psychology, 47,* 7–15.

76. Asch, S. (1955). Opinions and social pressure. *Scientific American, 193,* 31–35.

77. Cialdini, R.B., & Goldstein, N.J. (2004). Social influence: Compliance and conformity. In S.T. Fiske, D.L. Schacter & C. Zahn-Waxler (Eds), *Annual review of psychology* (Vol. 55, pp. 591–621). Palo Alto, CA: Annual Reviews.

78. Deutsch, M., & Gerard, H.B. (1955). A study of normative and informational social influences upon individual judgment. *Journal of Abnormal and Social Psychology, 51,* 629–636.

79. Brown, G., & Baer, M. (2011). Location in negotiation: Is there a home field advantage? *Organizational Behavior and Human Decision Processes,* 114:190–200.

80. Rubin, J.Z., & Brown, B.R. (1975). *The social psychology of bargaining and negotiations.* New York: Academic Press.

81. Dirks, K.T., & Ferrin, D.L. (2001). The role of trust in organizational settings. *Organization Science, 12,* 450–467.

82. Lewicki, R.J., McAllister, D.J., & Bies, R.J. (1998). Trust and distrust: New relationships and realities. *Academy of Management Review, 23*, 438–458.

83. Berg, J., Dickhaut, J., & McCabe, K. (1995). Trust, reciprocity, and social history. *Games and Economic Behavior, 10*, 122–142.

84. Pillutla, M.M., Deepak, M., & Murnighan, J.K. (2003). Attributions of trust and the calculus of reciprocity. *Journal of Experimental Social Psychology, 39*, 448–455.

85. Fehr, E., & Rockenbach, B. (2003). Detrimental effects of sanctions on human altruism. *Nature, 422*, 137–140.

86. Baumeister, R.F., Bratslavsky, E., Finkenauer, C., & Vohs, K.D. (2001). Bad is stronger than good. *Review of General Psychology, 5*, 323–370.

87. Kim, P., Ferrin, D., Cooper, C., & Dirks, K. (2004). Removing the shadow of suspicion: The effects of apology versus denial for repairing competence- versus integrity-based trust violations. *Journal of Applied Psychology, 89*, 104–118.

88. Haselhuhn, M.P., Schweitzer, M.E., & Wood, A.M. (2010). How implicit beliefs influence trust recovery. *Psychological Science, 21*, 645–648.

89. Tomlinson, E.C., Dineen, B.R., & Lewicki, R.J. (2004). The road to reconciliation: Antecedents of victim willingness to reconcile following a broken promise. *Journal of Management, 30*, 165–187.

90. Leunissen, J.M., De Cremer, D., & Reinders Folmer, C.P. (2012). An instrumental perspective on apologizing in bargaining: The importance of forgiveness to apologize. Journal of Economic Psychology, 33, 215–222.

91. Leunissen, J., De Cremer, D., Reinders Folmer, C.P., & Van Dijke, M. (2011). *Apologizing and self-esteem*. Rotterdam, The Netherlands: Rotterdam School of Management, Erasmus Universiteit.

92. Kim, P.H., Dirks, K.T., Cooper, C.D., & Ferrin, D.L. (2006). When more blame is better than less: The implications of internal vs. external attributions for the repair of trust after a competence- vs. integrity-based trust violation. *Organizational Behavior and Human Decision Processes, 99,* 49–65.

93. De Cremer, D., & Schouten, B. (2008). When apologies for injustice matter: The role of respect. *European Psychologist, 13,* 239–247.

94. De Cremer, D., Pillutla, M., & Reinders Folmer, C. (2011). How important is an apology to you? Forecasting errors in predicting the true value of apologies. *Psychological Science, 22,* 45–48.

95. Bottom, W., Daniels, S., Gibson, K.S., & Murnighan, J.K. (2002). When talk is not cheap: Substantive penance and expressions of intent in the reestablishment of cooperation. *Organization Science, 13,* 497–515.

96. Desmet, P., De Cremer, D., & Van Dijk, E. (2011). In money we trust? When financial compensations matter in repairing trust perceptions. *Organizational Behavior and Human Decision Processes, 114,* 75–86.

97. De Cremer, D. (2010). When financial compensations versus apologies matter after transgressions in bargaining: It depends on whether the transgression involved losses or gains. *Journal of Economic Psychology, 31,* 843–848.

98. Desmet, P., De Cremer, D., & Van Dijk, E. (2011). *When compensation is not enough: Restoring trust in individuals and groups.* Rotterdam, The Netherlands: Rotterdam School of Management, Erasmus Universiteit.

99. French, J.R.P., & Raven, B. (1959). The bases of social power. In D. Cartwright & A. Zander (Eds), *Group Dynamics* (pp. 150–167). New York: Harper & Row.

100. Epley, N., & Caruso, E.M. (2008). Perspective taking: Misstepping into others' shoes. In K.D. Markman,

W.M. Klein & J.A. Suhr (Eds), *Handbook of imagination and mental simulation* (pp. 297–311). New York: Psychology Press.

101. Galinsky, A.D., Magee, J.C., Inesi, M.E., & Gruenfeld, D.H. (2006). Power and perspectives not taken. *Psychological Science, 17*, 1068–1074.

102. Goodwin, S.A., Gubin, A., Fiske, S.T., & Yzerbyt, V. (2000). Power can bias impression formation: Stereotyping subordinates by default and by design. *Group Processes and Intergroup Relations, 3*, 227–256.

103. Keltner, D., Gruenfeld, D.H., & Anderson, C. (2003). Power, approach, and inhibition. *Psychological Review, 110*, 265–284.

104. Anderson, C., & Galinsky, A.D. (2006). Power, optimism, and risktaking. *European Journal of Social Psychology, 36*, 511–536.

105. Van Kleef, G.A., De Dreu, C.K.W., Pietroni, D., & Manstead, A.S.R. (2006). Power and emotion in negotiation: Power moderates the interpersonal effects of anger and happiness on concession making. *European Journal of Social Psychology, 36*, 557–581.

106. Tenbrunsel, A.E. (2005). Are you too powerful for your own good? *Negotiation, 8*(September), 1–4.

107. Lount, R.B. Jr., Zhong, C., Sivanathan, N., & Murnighan, J.K. (2008). Getting off on the wrong foot: The timing of a breach and the restoration of trust. *Personality and Social Psychology Bulletin, 34*, 1601–1612.

108. Reinders Folmer, C.P., & Van Lange, P.A.M. (2007). Why promises and threats need each other. *European Journal of Social Psychology, 37*, 1016–1031.

109. Babcock, L., & Loewenstein, G. (1997). Explaining bargaining impasse: The role of self-serving biases. *The Journal of Economic Perspectives, 11*, 109–126.

110. Pillutla, M., & Murnighan, J.K. (2003). Fairness in bargaining. *Social Justice Research, 16*(3), 241–262.

111. Deutsch, M. (1975). Equity, equality, and need: What determines which value will be used as the basis of distributive justice? *Journal of Social Issues, 31*(3), 137–150.

112. Adams, J.S. (1965). Inequity in social exchange. *Advances in Experimental Social Psychology, 2*, 267–299.

113. Messick, D.M., & Sentis, K. (1979). Fairness, and preference. *Journal of Experimental Social Psychology, 15*(4), 418–434.

114. Kapstein, E. (2008). Fairness considerations in world politics: Lessons from international trade negotiations. *Political Science Quarterly, 123*(2), 229–245.

115. Messick, D.M. (1993). Equality as a decision heuristic. In B.A. Mellers & J. Baron (Eds), *Psychological perspectives on justice* (pp. 11–31). New York: Cambridge University Press.

116. Giacobbe-Miller, J., Miller, D., & Zhang, W. (1997). Equity, equality and need as determinants of pay allocations: A comparative study of Chinese and US managers. *Employee Relations, 19*, 4.

BIOGRAPHY

David De Cremer is Professor of Management at China Europe International Business School (CEIBS), China. He was Professor of Behavioural and Business Ethics at the Rotterdam School of Management (RSM) at Erasmus University in the Netherlands and at the London Business School (LBS), UK, until mid-2012. He was also the research director at the Erasmus Centre of Behavioural Ethics in the Netherlands earlier. David holds an M.Sc. from the University of Leuven, Belgium, and a Ph.D. from the University of Southampton, UK. He has been a visiting professor/researcher at New York University and Harvard University – both in the USA. His research activities take place at the intersection between psychology, economics, and management and have been published in the top academic journals in psychology, organizational behaviour, and management. He has received numerous international distinctions and awards (from, amongst others, the European Association of Social Psychology, the European Federation of Psychology, the International Society of Justice Research, and the British Society of Psychology). In 2009–2010 he was named as the most influential economist in the Netherlands in the annual 'Top 40' list of leading economists. His research has been discussed in various publications, including the *Scientific American, Bloomberg News, The Economist*, and the *Financial Times*. He regularly contributes to financial–economic newspapers and magazines in Belgium, the Netherlands, and the

United Kingdom. In 2010 a number of these contributions appeared in the book *When Good People Do Bad Things: Illustrations of the Psychology behind the Financial Crisis.*

Madan M. Pillutla is the Mike Salamon Professor of Organizational Behaviour at the London Business School, UK, where he is also the director of the Negotiations and Influencing for Senior Managers open programme. Madan holds an undergraduate degree in engineering, graduate degrees in human resource management and organizational behaviour, and a doctorate in management from the University of British Columbia, Canada. Prior to coming to London Business School, he worked as an assistant professor at the Hong Kong University of Science and Technology, China, and as a personnel manager for ITC Limited, a subsidiary of British American Tobacco.

His research and award-winning teaching focuses on negotiations, influence, and behavioural decision-making. His research has been featured in most of the top academic publications such as the *Academy of Management Journal, Organizational Behavior and Human Decision Processes, Games and Economic Behavior*, and the *Journal of Marketing Research*. He is an associate editor of *Organizational Behavior and Human Decision Processes*, and serves on the editorial board of *Administrative Science Quarterly* and *Academy of Management Review*. Among his current research projects are an investigation into the origin of fair behaviour in exchange situations: that is, are we born with the capacity to be fair, or is it something we learn? Other research projects include an investigation into how people rebuild trust following transgressions in interpersonal relationships and the effect of ostracism on employee motivation and behaviour. Madan teaches negotiation and bargaining in a variety of MBA and executive programmes at the London Business School. He is active as a corporate trainer for a number of global corporations, including AVIVA, Deutsche Bank, Ericsson, Lloyds, and the United Nations Development Programme (UNDP).

INDEX

DATE DUE

			PRINTED IN U.S.A.